Plan & Go: The John Muir Trail

All you need to know to complete one of the world's greatest trails

Gerret Kalkoffen

sandiburg press

Plan & Go: The John Muir Trail

Copyright © 2014 by Gerret Kalkoffen

ISBN 978-0-692-20893-9

Editor: Kevin Muschter

Proofreader: Michael Schugardt

published by sandiburg press

Content

0. Preface

This book is meant to give you all the information you need to prepare for and successfully complete the John Muir Trail (JMT). I am convinced you will be well prepared and save a lot of time on planning if you read the following chapters.

The book's title is a reference to my approach to anything. I find it best to put generous thought into how I want to do something, plan, organize, and then get moving. I try to convey the most important hiking information in a short but comprehensive manner. If you are looking for elaborate stories on the JMT, its history, and details on flora and fauna, this is not the book for you. However, if you are toying with the idea of hiking the JMT or have already accepted the challenge and wonder how to prepare for it, then I hope this helps – both for inexperienced hikers as well as experts.

The setting of the JMT in the California High Sierra Mountains is breath-taking. Each day, you will experience new landscapes: lush meadows with grazing dear, clear streams sparkling amidst dark pine forests, or nothing but sun-burnt rocks and boulders. Throughout a long summer stretch, weather conditions will be very pleasant. It is absolutely worth taking a few weeks to experience the solitude and nature's beauty along the trail. I promise completing the JMT will be one of the greatest and most memorable experiences of your life.

1. Introduction

After months of witnessing me prepare – making travel arrangements, researching gear, reading forums, and working out – my wife said I should write a book. I snickered but kept that thought in the back of my mind while on the trail, noting each evening in my tent what worked well and what could have gone better. In conversations with fellow JMT hikers I realized that many experiences were shared and, especially, that many similar mistakes were reoccurring. With my aversion to repeating each other's mistakes, I decided that this repetition was unnecessary and my wife was – of course – right: passing on the experiences of how to prepare and what worked on the JMT would be of value to most anyone attempting this hike.

That's the story of how this book came to life. Now, here is the story of what it is about. The JMT is a 211mi/340km trail from Yosemite Valley to the highest point of the continental US, Mt. Whitney. From the top of Mt. Whitney, it is another 11mi/18km to the nearest trailhead at Whitney Portal.

The trail was named after John Muir, a Scottish conservationist and first president of the Sierra Club, a driving force behind this trail and other preservations[1]. In total, the JMT runs through five of the US' most picturesque national parks and offers spectacular sceneries of canyons, cliffs, forests, lakes, rivers, peaks and passes of over 14,000ft. It is one of the most renowned and widely recognized as one of the greatest trails in the world.

---

[1] www.sierraclub.org

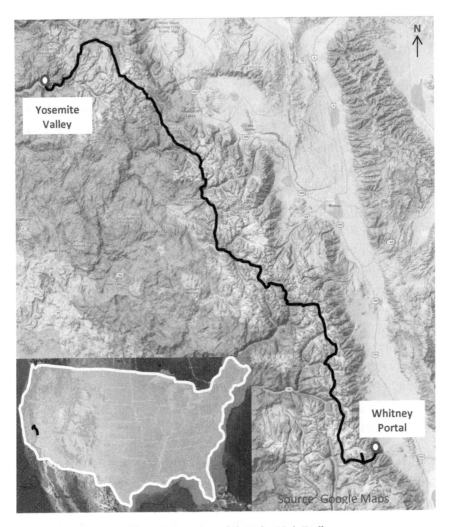

Figure 1 Overview of the John Muir Trail

Finally, here is how I came to hike the JMT. I had just moved to San Diego, California, with a vague idea of wanting to switch careers (i.e., I was not working and had time to spare). One of my best friends, Josh, was on a one-year sabbatical and looking for an adventure, despite having just walked 450mi/720km along the ancient pilgrimage route Camino de Santiago. He called me one day and asked if I had heard of the JMT. I said no, but looked into it and was stunned. Though I love hiking, I had never camped for more than 3 days in a row. I had consequently never dealt with planning large quantities of light weight food, fitting that food into a bear canister, and how to resupply myself via mail. I was also not familiar with the specifics of the High Sierra, how to treat water, how much of it to carry, and which gear and clothing were appropriate for the conditions. However, my initial concerns were put on hold when I saw pictures of the trail.

After a quick chat with Josh, we decided to go for it. I bought a book, read lots of blogs, several online forums, and the National Parks' websites. I soon learned that getting a wilderness permit would be the bottle neck, but we got lucky. As I continued my research, I grew more confident. I was gathering lots of answers to my early questions and reading up on trail descriptions. I found that the JMT would be the perfect amount of adventure: it is in remote wilderness areas, but is decently frequented by hikers, has occasional ranger stations and sporadic ins/outs to nearby towns. The more sources I combined, the better my picture of the JMT was and the more capable I felt of the challenge.

Essentially, that is why I wrote this book. I want you to have a clear picture of what to expect on the JMT and how best to prepare yourself. Chapter 2 describes the physical challenges of the trail and gives guidance on estimating the time it will take to complete it. This initial estimate of your trail hiking days allows you to prepare the Long Lead Items of Chapter 3, such as permits and travel plans. Chapter 4 lets you know what to expect regarding weather and trail conditions, campsites, and water. How to prepare for all this physically and logistically is the topic of Chapter 5. Then, Chapter 6 takes a close look at gear options for this High Sierra setting and their correct use. Finally, Chapter 7 offers some personal experiences and anecdotes from Josh's and my adventure. Additionally, the Appendices provide checklists, elevation profiles, side trip suggestions and more, to round-off your picture of and preparation for the hike.

I hope you will find all the information you need herein and feel confident to hike the JMT.

Happy Trails!

Visit www.planandgohiking.com for more pictures & posts

2. Requirements and Time

Can you hike the JMT? If you are interested in hiking and have some experience, the answer is probably yes. However, 222mi/360km with 47,800ft/14,600m gain and 43,200ft/13,200m loss reaching its highest point at 14,500ft/4.420m Mt. Whitney is a challenge for anyone[2].

General requirements on the trail are surefootedness, ability to deal with high altitudes, and a good overall level of fitness and endurance. However, since the JMT is maintained to be passed by horses, this is a non-technical trail, i.e. no climbing skills are needed. Nevertheless, in the winter months / when snow is present, special gear and skills are necessary for safe travels.

Further requirements for the logistics are a strong back and knees to carry the load of your backpack (approx. 30-45lb/14-20kg), resistance to dry air and both hot and cold temperatures, and the ability to camp (using a gas stove, setting up your tent and pad, following nature's call in the wild, etc.).

In order to have an adequate challenge, start by planning your days on the trail. As a first guideline, use Figure 2 - based on your age and fitness level. The chart is meant to help you with an initial assessment of how many days you will take for the JMT. This is the first step to all your further planning, especially regarding food and resupply.

Take the row with your age on the left and move right to the column corresponding to your level of fitness. For example, "John", a 40 year old of average fitness should plan to take roughly 16-18 days, so let us say 17.

---

[2] All distances and elevation gains/losses are from Yosemite Valley Happy Isles to Whitney Portal.

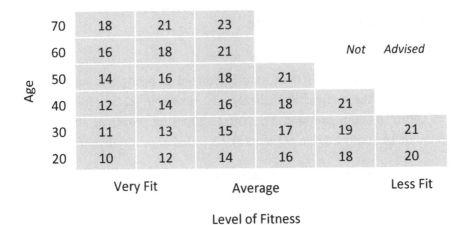

Age	Very Fit		Average			Less Fit
70	18	21	23			
60	16	18	21		*Not*	*Advised*
50	14	16	18	21		
40	12	14	16	18	21	
30	11	13	15	17	19	21
20	10	12	14	16	18	20

Level of Fitness

Figure 2 Estimate of Trail Days on the JMT

With your estimate of trail days (ETD), you can calculate your average miles per day: divide 222 miles by your ETD.

Average miles per day = 222 miles / ETD

Taking the above example of John leads to 222/17= 13 miles per day on average. That might not sound like much, but keep in mind that every horizontal mile is accompanied by 230ft up and 210ft down, i.e., equivalent to approx. 500 stair steps up and 450 steps down.

While on the JMT, I met a 74 year old who was planning 24 days with his wife; a 67 year old who was doing the JMT in 32 day (for the 8th time!); a 63 year old who finished in 16 days; and a 50 year old who completed the JMT in 15 days. On average, most people will spend 15-20 days between Yosemite and Whitney Portal. Schedules vary greatly on how each one allocates time on and off the trail, hiking and relaxing.

In order to account for these differences and to give you a more personalized trail itinerary, consider the following questions:

Would you like to do any side trips? (See Appendix D)
- if yes, add one day to your ETD for every multiple of your average miles per day.

> In our example, if John wants to do a total of 15 miles of side trips, he adds 1 (=15 / 13) days to his ETD. His new ETD is 17 + 1 = 18

Would you like to go fishing?
- yes, if it works within the schedule = add 0
- yes, every now and then = multiply your ETD by 1.1
- yes, wherever possible = multiply your ETD by 1.3

> In our example, John likes to go fishing every now and then. His side trips are also fishing related. His new ETD is 18 x 1.1 = 20

Would you like to take extra time along the trail to stop at lakes, meadows, etc. for animal watching, relaxing, or other?
- if yes, add the multiple of half/ days you would like to take as extra time to your ETD

> In our example, John thinks fishing is good enough for him. He will try to integrate stops at lakes and meadows with fishing and food breaks. He adds 0 to his ETD.

Do you plan on eating out along the trail?
- yes, where convenient (e.g. Reds Meadows) : add nothing
- yes, especially at Vermillion Resort : add 1 day to your ETD

> In our example, John had forgotten about Vermillion. He has all other stops and side trips planned. Just for Vermillion, he adds one day to his ETD. His total days on the trail is 21.

With your ETD from the Figure 2 and the additional questions, calculate your total days on the trail. This should be the basis for all your future planning regarding travel, food, and resupply.

If you cannot answer these questions yet, do not worry. You may only know whether or not you would like to go on side trips after further investigations. Maybe even then, you will not know exactly how much time to spend where, but you will be aware of the possibilities, know to plan for (spontaneous) extra days in the northern half where resupplying is easier, and/or pack some extra food.

3. Long Lead Items

a. Permits

Hiking the JMT requires a wilderness permit[3]. In total, the JMT runs through five national park jurisdictions. Luckily, one permit is valid for your entire journey. You have a few options regarding your entry point to the JMT, but all trailheads require a wilderness permit.

As your entry permit will determine your direction, here are a few things to consider:

Entry from the North, hiking South:
- The vast majority of hikers walk north to south, hence you will bump into less people
- You avoid the Mt. Whitney permit lottery
- By the time you reach Mt. Whitney, you are well adjusted to high altitudes
- You can opt to start light, as there are resupply stations early along the trail

Entry from the South, hiking North:
- The sun mostly hits your back, rather than your face
- Transportation upon arrival in Yosemite is easier
- Given the risk of a shortened trip, you saw the remarkable Mt. Whitney

Regarding further thoughts on transportation and logistics, please see Chapters 3c *Travel Arrangements* for details and consider 3b *Hiking Buddy* to see for how big of a group you need to get the permit.

---

[3] I am fully aware that this is a wildly uninteresting subject, but I did not want to bump it into the Appendices, because it is one of the first things you need to tackle in order to hike the JMT. Once you've decided on a direction, it is a straight forward deal.

Once you have chosen your preferred direction, check to see which trailhead permits are still available and suit your travel plans. You need not worry about the length of your hike (your total ETD); though you will be asked an estimated exit date, it is not binding.

If you plan on hiking the entire JMT in one go you have only two permit options: Happy Isles via Little Yosemite Valley or Mt. Whitney; these are the official start/end points of the JMT. If you want to hike approx. the same distance as the JMT but can live with an initial small detour, Yosemite Valley offers two good alternatives: Happy Isles via Sunrise or Glacier Point via Panorama Trail. These two trails bring you to the JMT after a few miles where they detour the heavily frequented stretch that is used by Half Dome day hikers. In the south, there is only one alternative to Mt. Whitney: the Kearsarge Pass via Onion Valley. However, this 7.3mi/11.7km trail only merges with the JMT approx. at the 180mi/290km mark from Yosemite, cutting the JMT short by over 30mi/48km.

Yosemite Valley
In Yosemite, there are three easy entry options to the JMT:
1. Happy Isles   → Little Yosemite Valley
2. Happy Isles   → Sunrise/Merced Lake (pass through)
3. Glacier Point → Little Yosemite Valley

The most popular trailhead of all by far is Yosemite's Happy Isles trailhead with permit to Little Yosemite Valley. This is, however, also most likely to be fully booked shortly after reservations open. Go to [Yosemite Permits][4] and check the "full trailheads report" for availability. Permits can (and should!) be reserved 24 weeks / 168 days in advance via fax, phone, or mail. Only 60 percent of all permits can be reserved. The remaining 40 percent are first-come, first-serve and are available the day before trail entry at the Yosemite Valley Wilderness Center which opens at 7:30am (July & August) or 8:00 (rest of year).

---

[4] [ ] indicates Internal Reference, please see Appendix E

If you are starting at Glacier Point, you can choose to hike up from the valley floor via Four-Mile Trail or take a charter bus. Starting from the valley, take a public [YARTS] bus to the Four-Mile Trailhead. From there, it is 4.8mi/7.4km with a steep incline to Glacier Point. Alternatively, you can take a one-way charter bus ride starting at Yosemite Lodge for $25 per adult, departing daily at 8:30am, 10am and 1:30pm and taking approx. 1½ hours. Please check times and reserve in advance [Glacier Point Bus]. From Glacier Point, it is an easy to moderate hike along the Panorama Trail past Nevada Fall to the JMT, with stunning views of Yosemite Valley and Half Dome.

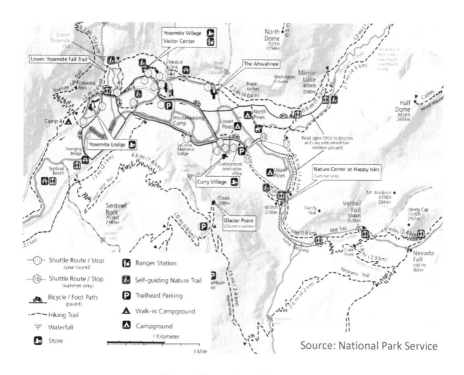

Source: National Park Service

Figure 3 Yosemite Valley Map

After having picked up your permit from the Wilderness Center, you are allowed one overnight stay the night before your entry date at the backpackers' campground in Yosemite Valley. It is between Tenaya Creek and the main bike path, just north of North Pines campground. Bear bins and toilets are located on site, $10 campground fee per adult, cash paid in an envelope on site. As the JMT officially ends at the top of Mt. Whitney, the JMT permit starting at Yosemite explicitly includes the summit.

Whitney Portal - Inyo National Forest

Entering from Mt. Whitney, you cannot reserve a permit but must participate in a lottery if you are planning your trip between May 1 through November 1. Lottery applications are accepted from February 1 to March 15. 100 percent of day use and overnight permits can be reserved. Space is not saved for walk-in permits; however, some openings from cancelations may be available just before the date. There is no wait list for cancelations. One or two days before your trip you must pick up your permit or confirm your group size to hold the permit for late arrival. Hikers must pick up their permit at the Eastern Sierra InterAgency Visitor Center in Lone Pine.

A $6.00 transaction fee and a $15 per person reservation fee will apply and are non-refundable for all Mt. Whitney reservations. Check [Mt. Whitney Permits].

Standing on the highest point of the entire continental US is quite an experience. Alternatively, you can enter via Inyo National Forest without summiting Mt. Whitney, hence avoiding the lottery. You can consider:

Permit issued by Inyo National Forest, Mt. Whitney Ranger District

- Kearsarge Pass (Onion Valley): Moderate. Access to John Muir Trail near Charlotte Lake, approx. 180mi/290km from Yosemite. First campsite - Flower Lake (3.5 mi/5.6 km). Limit 60 people/day.

Permits issued by Inyo National Forest, White Mountain Ranger District

- Piute Pass (North Lake): Moderate to strenuous. Access to John Muir Trail, Evolution Valley. First campsite - Lock Leven (3.5 mi/5.6 km). Limit 32 people/day.

- Bishop Pass (South Lake): Moderate to strenuous. Access to Dusy Basin. First campsite - Long Lake (3 mi/4.8 km). Limit 36 people/day.

Access to the JMT via Piute and Bishop Pass is so central that they do not serve well as initial trailheads, but are rather convenient if you plan on hiking the JMT in multiple sessions.

Sierra National Forest
Florence Lake Trail past Muir Trail Ranch is also a good re-entry/exit point if you wish to section the JMT. As it is around half way between the JMT's north and south ends, it is not especially suitable as a starting point.

- Florence Lake Trail (Florence Lake): Moderate. Access to Evolution Valley and Goddard Canyon. First campsite - Blaney Meadow (10mi/16km) A boat-taxi is available from Florence Lake trailhead in the summer. Visit www.muirtrailranch.com

60 percent of all permits can be reserved up to one year in advance. The remaining 40 percent are available the day before entry at the wilderness station [Sierra National Forest Permits].

Similar to Florence Lake Trail, the Vermillion Trailhead at Lake Edison via Mono Creek Trail is a good re-entry/exit point.

- Vermillion / Mono Creek Trailhead (Lake Edison): Easy to moderate. Access to JMT at Quail Meadows (4.8mi/7.7km). Good view of the lake, surrounding meadow and forest.

There is a ferry that runs twice daily, leaving Vermillion Valley Resort at 9:00am and 4:00pm. It stops at the northeast end of the lake near the Mono Creek trail entrance to the John Muir Wilderness. There is a fee for the ferry service.

! Be advised that the ferry may not operate throughout the entire summer due to low water levels.

The trail is subject to permitting and quotas apply from May 1 to November 1. During this time check with [High Sierra Ranger District].

Sequoia / Kings Canyon National Park
Sequoia / Kings Canyon NP offers some of the most remote access to the JMT.

Outside the quota period, which is usually end of September until end of May, wilderness permits are NOT limited to daily entry quotas and are free. However, for the purpose of Search and Rescue incidents, permits must be obtained at the proper issuing locations.

During the quota season, usually end of May until end of September, there is a $15 wilderness permit fee for overnight trips per group. The permits are issued for the trailhead where you begin your trip and must be obtained from the permit station closest to your trailhead.

Go to [Sequoia / Kings Canyon National Park] to get the permit application form and a list of the issuing locations.

The most relevant permit issued by Sequoia / Kings Canyon NP Road's End Permit Station is for

- Bubbs Creek Trail (Road's End): Steep then steady grade. Access to JMT near Rae Lakes, 168mi/270km from Yosemite Valley.

b. Hiking Buddy

Finding the right hiking buddy for this challenging endeavor can be a challenge in itself. Depending on who your friends are, this part may be complicated or not. Either way, your prospective hiking buddy[5] will need sufficient time to prepare, so you need to think about who you want to give a heads up. But before you start asking everyone you know, you may want to consider this:

- You will be spending 2+ weeks with this person, day and night
- You should have somewhat similar hiking speeds
  - Do your age / fitness levels match?
  - Do you have similar attitudes and interests?
  - Will you / will your buddy be taking a lot of photos, want to fish, or other?
- Your buddy should be likely to keep his commitment

After you tell your friends about your idea – and they hear the three letters "JMT" for the first time in their lives – allow each other time to think about it. Your prospective trail mates should honestly and critically assess, whether they are capable of the challenge. If they are passionate, they will make it happen and the 24 weeks of advance registration will be enough time for them to prepare. However, if either of you have doubts, discuss them openly. If it is not meant to be, it is best to sort that out before hitting the trail.

Regarding gear and supplies, travelling alone or with others makes a difference, but not a huge one. Usually, you can share a stove, pot, water purifier, first aid kit, pocket knife, emergency rope, map, shovel, and a camera. This adds up to approx. 4lb/2kg. So with one buddy, you save 2lb/1kg, with 4 buddies, you save 3lb/1,5kg. At an average pack weight of 44lb/20kg, traveling alone means an additional weight of not quite 10% more than if you were traveling in a group of 4, and 5% more

---

[5] For simplicity, I am using the male, singular form "hiking buddy", which shall also include all female and multiple "buddies" if applicable.

than if you were travelling with one buddy.

Of most things, however, each of you will need or want your own (see Chapter 6 *Gear*). Though sharing a tent would also save some weight, it does not outweigh the comfort of being able to retreat alone after a long day.

Especially if this is your first multi-day hike, a friend by your side can keep spirits up and make recovering easier. You can help keep each other on schedule, discuss how far to walk, where to set up camp, where to rest, remind each other to put on sun screen, etc. In case of an emergency, it is obviously good to have someone close. Though the JMT is quite frequented in the summer time, you never know when another hiker will pass.

For several other reasons, it is wonderful to bring a companion. As you will usually only pass-by a few people (asking the standard questions "Where is the next water?", "Where are good camp sites?"), your conversations on the trail will be limited. Occasional chats, bursts of ideas, philosophical ramblings, and other peak-sun streaks of genius are always nice to get off ones chest. And recalling the stunning scenery and animals you passed while waiting for the water to boil at camp will help engrave the impressions of that day even deeper. Furthermore, the shared memories will stay with you for life.

Nonetheless, many people cannot or do not want to find a hiking buddy and will go solo. To some, the pool of potential companions is limited, given the physical and time requirements. Others make a conscious decision to journey alone, test their strength, soul-search, or genuinely experience the solitude. Hiking the JMT alone is a viable option and quite common. All gear and supplies can be carried alone and the way the JMT is frequented (in summer) assistance in case of an emergency can usually be expected within reasonable time. If you are starting alone but hope to join/form a group, hiking the predominant direction north-to-south greatly increases your options.

c. Travel Arrangements

Getting to and from the main trailheads at Yosemite Valley and Whitney Portal takes some planning, but is still rather convenient when you consider that you are entering a wilderness zone. Depending on where you are coming from and which direction you want to walk the JMT, choose a combination of the below means of transportation and make sure to check the schedules [Travel Arrangements].

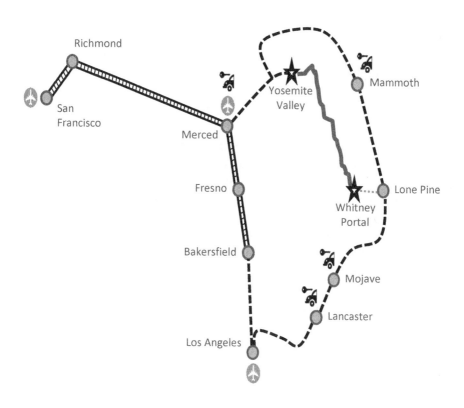

Figure 4 Map Overview of Travel Options

San Francisco (International Airport - SFO) to Merced

Take Bay Area Rapid Transit (BART) to Richmond (red line direct or yellow to 19th St. Oakland and transfer to orange). In Richmond, transit onto Amtrak train 7xx[6] San Joaquin South. Exit in Merced (Amtrak Station).
Travel time approx. 3½h; Cost approx. $ 35

Los Angeles (Union Station Amtrak) to Merced

Take Amtrak Bus 58xx to Bakersfield. Exit in Bakersfield and transfer to Amtrak train 7xx San Joaquin North. Exit in Merced (Amtrak Station).
Travel time approx. 3h; Cost approx. $ 45

Merced to Yosemite Valley

Take Yosemite Area Regional Transportation System (YARTS) Blue Line bus from airport / rental car center or Amtrak station to Yosemite Valley.
Travel time approx. 2½h; Cost approx. $ 15

Los Angeles (Union Station Metrolink) to Lone Pine

Take Metrolink 207 Antelope Valley Line Train to Lancaster. Exit in Lancester and transit onto Eastern Sierra Transit Bus 395 to Mammoth Lakes or Reno. Exit at Lone Pine. Be aware that buses may run very infrequently – especially on the 395 route. They may not run at all on weekends and/or only every other day. Keep this in mind for both your start and finish dates.
Travel time approx. 6h; Cost approx. $ 40

Lone Pine to Yosemite Valley

Take Eastern Sierra Transit Bus 395 to Mammoth Lakes, Mammoth Express, or Reno. Exit at Mammoth Lakes. Walk 100ft/30m to Main St. / Shilo Inn bus station. Transit onto Yosemite Area Regional Transportation System (YARTS) Green Line Bus towards Yosemite Valley. Exit within Yosemite Valley as needed.
Travel time approx. 5¾ h; Cost approx. $ 35

Whitney Portal to Lone Pine

If Whitney Portal is your JMT exit, you will probably find several hikers that are willing to give you a ride to Lone Pine. Alternatively, you can ask

---

[6] "xx" depends on time and day

at the Whitney Portal Shop and Restaurant to call you a shuttle as needed. If Whitney is your starting point, you can pre-book a shuttle. Various operators offer shuttle services. Just search the term "lone pine shuttle service".

Travel time approx. ½h; Cost depends on number of people (or free)

Lone Pine to Los Angeles

Take Eastern Sierra Transit Bus 395 and Metrolink 207 as described above. Alternatively, you can also try your thumb-luck standing at the corner of Main St. and Whitney Portal Rd. People in Lone Pine are used to hikers in need. Irregular service, not every day.

Travelling by rental car

Renting a car can save you a lot of time if public transport connections are unfortunate for your location and/or date of travel. The closest rental car centers to the trail heads are Merced, Mammoth, Mojave, and Lancaster. Each has at least one major rental car agency that allows one-way rentals and is also accessible via bus or train. Make sure to pre-book your car and check for office hours.

Travelling by airplane

Most out-of-state hikers will fly into San Francisco or Los Angeles. Any combination of the above buses, trains, and rental cars is then easily available. Additionally, there are regular scheduled flights between Los Angeles-Merced and Las Vegas-Merced. There is both a rental car office as well as a YARTS bus stop at Merced airport.

Travelling with your own car

There is long-term parking at both trailheads, so you can choose to leave your car at your start or finishing point. After strenuous weeks of hiking, being able to get in your car and take off without having to worry about bus connections can be worth getting the logistics over with before starting your trek. Remember not to leave any food or scented items in your car.

Having a cell phone charger that plugs into your lighter outlet may come in handy.

4. What to Expect

This Chapter is intended to give you an impression of the conditions on the JMT. This can serve as a guide to choosing your gear and making your preparations. Later, you can compare your thoughts with a gear overview in Chapter 6 *Gear* and my personal experiences in Chapter 7 *Plan* and *Go*.

a. Weather & Conditions

Temperature

The most important measure in deciding what kind of clothing to bring is the expected temperature. In order to estimate temperatures along the trail, it is useful to use a lapse rate. As a rule of thumb, deduct 5°F per every 1,000ft or 10°C per every 1,000m of gain in altitude in the respective month you are planning your trip. Use Table 1 below with data from Yosemite Valley at 4,000ft/1,220m.

Month	°F	°C
	(min/max)	(min/max)
January	29 / 48	-2 / 9
February	30 / 52	-1 / 11
March	34 / 58	1 / 14
April	38 / 64	3 / 18
May	45 / 72	7 / 22
June	51 / 81	11 / 27
July	57 / 89	14 / 32
August	56 / 89	13 / 32
September	51 / 82	11 / 28
October	42 / 71	6 / 22
November	33 / 56	1 / 13
December	28 / 47	-2 / 8

Source: US National Park Service
Table 1 Average Temperatures in Yosemite Valley (4,000ft/1,220m)

For example, in °F and feet: If you plan to start in July in Yosemite Valley (at 4,000ft), you can expect temperatures of 57-89°F. As you reach

Tuolumne Meadows (at approx. 9,000ft) after a few days, the temperature band will have dropped by ((9,000ft – 4,000ft)/1,000ft) * 5°F = 25°F to 32-64°F. After further hiking up to passes over 12,000ft, your maximum temperature may only be around 50°F. However, you will rarely camp above 10,000ft; there, your temperature band is 27-59°F.

If you are hiking between June and August, prepare for spending the majority of your days in temperatures of 50-70°F / 10-20°C during the day and 25-50°F / -4-10°C at night. Though it is hard to imagine when you are climbing sweat-drenched out of Yosemite Valley or up from Whitney Portal at 90°F / 30°C, only two days later your sleeping bag can be securely frozen to your tent – like mine was. As you ascend, you are likely to pass patches of snow still in August. The changes in temperature are astonishing and require both light and airy day clothes as well as insulated warm evening clothing.

Remember that you will be at altitudes well above 9,000ft for a great portion of the trail. This means that while temperatures may be fairly low during the day, due to low humidity and aerosols, the sun will be merciless. At the same time, this source of warmth will set early behind other peaks and temperatures will drop quickly. Additionally, any water you find for washing clothes and yourself will likely be around 40-60°F / 4-15°C. Keep this in mind when planning your arrivals to camp. At the end of a long day, your energy and body heat fade. And while you will want to wash off dust and sweat, regaining a comfortable temperature becomes a challenge after sunset. This means, the earlier you can set out in the morning, the more distance you can cover before the sun is too hot, but also arrive at camp and get washed up while the sun is still out and strong enough to dry/warm you.

Precipitation

From June to September, when most hikers hit the trail, it will only rain occasionally – if at all. However, there is a fair chance that it will rain at least once while you are hiking, especially in June (see Table 2).

Table 2 reads as follows: Taking the row of July: July has an average precipitation of 0.3in./1cm, historically wet Julys reached up to

4.2in./11cm; there is usually one day of rainfall of greater than 0.01in./0.3cm and one with more than 0.1in./3mm; there are zero days with any stronger precipitation let alone snowfall. So in a nutshell, July is a very dry month, as are June, August, and September.

	Precipitation in Yosemite Valley					Total Snowfall	
	Mean in.	High in.	≥ .01 in. # Days	≥ .10 in. # Days	≥ .50 in. # Days	Mean in.	High in.
Jan	6,5	24,6	9,0	8,0	4,0	16,2	140,8
Feb	6,2	22,6	9,0	7,0	4,0	14,6	89,0
Mar	5,4	21,0	10,0	8,0	4,0	12,9	67,0
Apr	3,0	12,1	7,0	5,0	2,0	5,1	81,0
May	1,5	7,9	5,0	3,0	1,0	0,2	3,0
Jun	0,7	4,0	3,0	2,0	0,0	0,0	0,0
Jul	0,3	4,2	1,0	1,0	0,0	0,0	0,0
Aug	0,2	1,4	1,0	1,0	0,0	0,0	0,0
Sep	0,7	5,2	2,0	2,0	0,0	0,0	0,0
Oct	1,9	10,7	4,0	3,0	1,0	0,2	4,0
Nov	3,9	15,1	6,0	5,0	3,0	3,6	59,0
Dec	6,0	29,6	8,0	7,0	4,0	12,5	59,0
Ann	36,3	68,9	68,0	51,0	24,0	65,3	154,9

Source: Western Regional Climate Center

Table 2 Precipitation at Yosemite Park Headquarters (1905-2012)

The amount of rain can vary from a brief downpour to a light drizzle over hours. As clouds start to form, it is good to get your light rain jacket readily available at the top of your pack. Remember, when seeking shelter during a thunderstorm, move away from freestanding trees and place your pack and other metal objects at a distance. Avoid peaks and passes and stay low to the ground among scattered boulders or trees.

As for weather patterns, "it never rains at night in the Sierra" seems to be mostly valid. After long stretches of clear skies, clouds may appear and often build up during the next days while vanishing at night. With every day your chances of getting wet increase. At the same time, heavy rain or even hail at night is possible, especially when a late summer / autumn storm rolls in. Be aware of your camp surrounding when this does happen and prepare to seek shelter away from the metal in your tent.

For reference, the temperature and precipitation data for the Mt. Whitney side of the JMT is very similar:

"Ninety five percent of total precipitation (which includes both rain and snow) falls between the months of October and May, with more than half falling in January, February, and March. The frequency of summer showers increase at higher elevations and correspondingly there are more cloudy days. But even though these thundershowers are of short duration they are still a danger to the hiker/climber on the summit or high ridges on Mt Whitney and other Sierra Peaks. That being said, if you detect a thunderstorm developing, vacate the summit and high ridges at once. The first recorded fatality on Mt Whitney was due to lightning." [7]

Looking at both temperature and precipitation explains why it is most busy and desirable to hike from June to September.

Other Conditions

Wild fires are unpredictable but common occurrences in California. Most recently in 2013, forest fires devastated large areas in the Yosemite Wilderness as well as around Mammoth. The fires never got close enough to the JMT to pose an immediate threat to hikers, but the partially thick smoke put stress on breathing and reduced visibility.

While you cannot prepare in advance for a wild fire, you can take the right precautions if you are aware of wild fires in the area. Call the ranger station or permit office closest to your trail head before leaving for your journey. Then, on the trail, ask hikers coming your way and stop at the scattered ranger stations to inquire about the status of the fires. If you experience shortness of breath, chest pain, rapid heart rate or

---

[7] http://timberlinetrails.net/WhitneyWeather.html

fatigue, take a break. Adjust your hiking distances for the next days or consider exiting the trail and continuing your adventure another time.

Another unpredictable, yet fortunately not so common occurrence is a government shutdown. Most recently in 2013, a 16-day federal shutdown forced over 400 national parks to close their gates in the first half of October. During that time, access roads to trail heads were closed as were permit issuing stations. In the event of such a shutdown, there is nothing you can do.

All in all, however, you will find little to no mountain ranges with as beautiful scenery and such stable weather conditions. The majority of your trail days will be lovely, hiker-friendly, and most enjoyable.

b. Trails

The JMT is wonderful. It is mostly a somewhat narrow, single lane trail that feels like a minimal disruption to the surrounding wilderness. As the trail is frequented (scarcely) by horses and mules, there is never a need for climbing (involving your hands). However, there are very steep, winding passages with sudden drop-offs to the sides, where you wonder how these large animals do it. The drop-offs and ledges also call for you to be fairly resistant to heights.

The predominant surfaces you walk on are well compacted dirt, gravel, and rock. However, the rock can vary from large slabs of immovable granite or basalt to loosely touching small boulders that shift under your step. Loose gravel or even sand and dust, on the other hand, may provide soft resistance as you push forward. Consequently, conditions on the trail can range from dry and dusty, to slippery when wet or muddy. Surefootedness is a must.

The slope of the trail is usually anything but flat. A look at the elevation maps (Appendix C) shows sections of gradual inclines and declines, as well as short and extended stretches of steep uphill and downhill treks. The steep, extended parts are usually turned into switchbacks while the many short ones are aided with steps.

While the JMT is usually easy to follow, direction markers are somewhat scarce. For the most part, there is only one trail to choose from, but frequently merging and diverging trails will have you checking your map repeatedly. Depending on the remoteness of the JMT section, these side trails and corresponding day hikers are more or less seldom. There will hardly be crowds of people, but there are some popular spots with easy access via day hike.

Early in the summer, there may be some wet river crossings as the abundance of melting snow fills the streams. However, most rivers have stepping stones, logs, or bridges to get you across on dry foot. Trekking poles or a walking stick come in especially handy when on shaky boulders amidst the rivers. Starting in July, most or all river crossings should be dry.

The tree line reaches far up the Sierras. Nonetheless, large stretches of your high alpine journey will be in little- or non-forested areas. The open trails provide panoramic views and an idea of what is ahead. At the same time, this means shade is a luxury. The higher up and the later in the summer, the California sun becomes ever more scorching and brutal. Prepare for a sun's intensity you have never experienced before.

c. Campsites

Regulations

Park services and common sense command you to use established campsites. These campsites are neither marked nor equipped with a picnic bench. They are simply flattened patches that should be in accordance with the selection guidelines (i.e. not on vegetation and at least 100ft away from water and trails). However, if you find an established campsite that does not meet the required distances, it may still be reasonable to use it instead of flattening other vegetation. Established campsites are plentiful along the JMT, giving you a wide variety of spots to choose from.

Wood campfires are only allowed in pre-existing fire rings. Generally, campfires are prohibited above 9,600ft in Yosemite, above 10,000ft in John Muir and Ansel Adams Wilderness as well as in San Joaquim and Kings Canyon National Park, and above 11,200ft in Sequoia National Park. There are some additional local restrictions and there may be strict "no fire" rules for all altitudes in times of drought. That said, refraining from campfires altogether – decreasing the risk of wild fires and conserving the limited timber – has a strong advocacy.

Choosing a Campsite

When choosing a campsite, consider two factors: climate and strategy.

Climate will be the more important factor. Remember to avoid camping in basins and dips as cold air sinks and gathers there. Likewise, moisture and dew collect the closer and level you are to water. This can lead to soaked gear or a solid layer of ice on your tent overnight. Moving just a few steps up and away from such cold-wet-air sinks can make for a much more comfortable night. It can also spare you some mosquito trouble. At the same time, you want to have reasonably easy access to water for washing and cooking. Otherwise, prepare accordingly before making camp and bring extra water. Ideally, your campsite will also provide wind shelter while allowing the sun to shine brightly from the east to warm and dry your tent and sleeping bag in the morning. Furthermore, choose dry sand or small gravel over any organic substance and vegetation - not only because it protects the environment but also because it contains less moisture that will creep into your tent from underneath. You will notice that many of the established campsites have a good balance of these factors and provide excellent places to rest.

Strategy plays a role in choosing your campsite along the way with regard to daily distances and strenuous segments. You will find that certain areas at the foot of a steep incline will have numerous existing campsites. This way, the ascent the next morning is not yet exposed to the hot sun while the easy downhill segment is in the afternoon. For considerations regarding daily distances, see the next Chapter 5a *Your Itinerary*.

d. Water

There is plenty. Even in late August, after three months of hardly any rain, the abundant snowfalls of winter and spring still feed the countless rivers and lakes. Large parts of the JMT lead you right along beautiful bodies of water – babbling in brooks or lying peaceful, mirroring the peaks. You rarely walk for more than one hour before a stream crosses your path. So water availability is not an issue.

While the waters look clear, they may be contaminated. The global prevalence of the protozoan Giardia lamblia and the E.coli bacteria does not stop in the Sierra Nevada. Both lead to diarrhea and abdominal cramps, sometimes with a delay of 5-15 days post exposure. Fortunately, both can be filtered and/or killed with common treatment methods (see Chapter 6d *Food & Drinks*). Equally important, however, is a good camp hygiene to limit the spread of microbe-borne illness – especially after a squat with a view.

In order to not to add to the problem, make sure to always bury human waste a minimum of 6in. below the surface. Additionally, everywhere along the JMT you are required to pack out toilet paper; it is often dug up and spread by animals in search of food. A zip lock bag is sufficient. Keep a distance of at least 100ft to any campsites, trails, and sources of water when choosing your loo. This is the best precaution to further contamination.

All National Park Services recommend treating any water you consume. If you decide not to treat your water, or even if you do, flowing rivers and especially side streams from steep slopes with little wildlife – let alone cattle – are least (likely to be) contaminated. When washing yourself, clothes, or dirty dishes, take some water and move at least 30ft/10m away from the river or lake. Make sure that neither soap nor leftover food enters the water. Biodegradable and organic soap is best, but even this must not be introduced to water as it destroys the surface tension.

5. Preparation & Planning

Congratulations! If you are still reading, you have not been discouraged by some of the hardship any multi-day backpacking journey may bring. While the remoteness of the JMT provides spectacular sceneries, it also calls for some advanced preparation, but nothing unmanageable. And rest assured that it is worth it – good preparation will make your hike all the more enjoyable, allowing you to fully submerge in the vast, peaceful mountains.

a. Your Itinerary

Macro-Planning

The below flow chart visualizes the first steps in planning your overall trip.

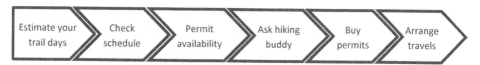

Figure 5 Flow Chart Macro Planning

As described in Chapter 3 *Long Lead Items*, the most important item to secure in advance is a trail permit. In order to know for when to get a permit it is good to know how long you estimate to take for your trip, when would be a good time for you, and when other hiking buddies are available. Most people commence their adventure between June and August when conditions are best.

Permits at Yosemite will be available as early as 24 weeks (168 days) prior to your entry date.

Desired trail entry in Yosemite	First day to make a reservation
May 1	Dec 2
Jun 1	Dec 15
Jul 1	Jan 14
Aug 1	Feb 14
Sep 1	Mar 17

Table 3 Advance for Permit Reservation in Yosemite

Similarly, lottery applications for permits starting at Whitney Portal are accepted from February 1 to March 15. Remember, while 100% of all permits are lottery-drawn for Mt. Whitney, only 60% of permits at Yosemite can be reserved in advance. So if you were not able to secure a permit in time, you can head up to Yosemite Valley and try your luck early in the morning at the Wilderness Center. If you are weather resistant, i.e. not afraid of the cold or rain, you can also aim for off-peak before or after June-August. The trail will present itself in ever greater solitude, but will also require better gear and greater skill when navigating snow-covered trails.

Once you have a permit and your ETD you have a start and end date. Now you can think about travel arrangements. Especially if you are coming from out of state or another country and need accommodations along the way, bear in mind that you will be in tourist-flocked California during peak season. Get started on flight, hotel/motel, car rental, and other bookings as soon as possible.

Micro-Planning

In order to have enough food up to and after resupply[8] and make it to the trail's end in time to catch your bus or rental car, your master itinerary and ETD need to be broken down into specific campsite goals along the trail.

For example, let us say your ETD was 22 days and you did not plan any side trips. 222mi/360km in 22 days means an average of 10mi/16km per day. However, there will be slow and fast days due to the terrain; so consistently aiming for 10mi/16km per day is not wise. Instead, use the distance-elevation profiles in Appendix C and mark your resupply spot/s, see example Figure 6 (in feet and miles). For more information on your resupply options, check Chapter 5d *Resupply*.

Sticking with the example, say you plan just one resupply at Muir Trail Ranch. Muir Trail Ranch is 0,9 miles from the JMT cut-off which is at mile 105 from Happy Isles. This already tells you that the one-stop resupply strategy is defiantly stretching it or impossible. At approx. 10mi/16km per day, it will take 10 days to reach Muir Trail Ranch – and one will hardly fit more than a 8-9-day food supply in a bear canister. Consequently, a 22 ETD split into two portions of 11 days of food is very borderline and requires excellent choice and packing of food. An alternative could be to send one resupply package to Reds Meadow Resort at mile 57 and a second one to Muir Trail Ranch at mile 106. But remember, regardless of what happens before Muir Trail Ranch, there are still 116 miles beyond it.

For the further planning, mark your average daily miles consecutively on the distance-elevation profile. Start with the first segment from Happy Isles (or your respective trailhead) to Reds Meadow Ranch (or your respective first resupply). With a pencil, lightly draw a mark each x-miles

---

[8] Resupply used in its singular form for simplicity, shall include multiple resupplies if applicable.

(your daily average, 10 miles sticking to the example) – these will be potential campsite areas.

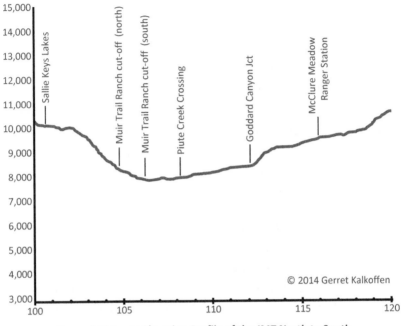

Figure 6 Distance-Elevation Profile of the JMT North to South

Make sure the total of your daily distances match when you should reach your resupply. Now, assess each mark on the elevation profile and make sure it is neither on a steep incline or decline, nor on a peak or in a basin. Furthermore, look at a topographic map to see surrounding profiles, access to water, and especially vicinity to hot springs. Shift the marks by a mile or two if the initial marks were in difficult terrain. However, make sure this does not lead to any day sections that are more than 20% longer than your daily average (i.e. 12 miles in our example), unless there is an unusually flat or gradual downhill section.

Repeat this process of roughly marking and reassessing campsites with the distance-elevation profile and topographic map for each section. When your markings to the distance-elevation profile are final you can transfer the markings into your map, as you will most likely be using this on the trail. Of course, they will only be approximate campsite locations, but this way you have an excellent measure for staying on track with your macro planning.

Use caution when planning side trips and be sure to factor them in correctly as they will not appear on the distance-elevation profile.

b. Athletic Training

For many readers the JMT will be their greatest adventure to date – and their greatest physical challenge. Don't be afraid to accept the challenge! With a decent level of fitness and the right mindset, you will revel in your accomplishment and soon seek the next.

Hiking Style
In order for you to use your energy efficiently and keep strains to your joints and tendons at a minimum, it is useful to adopt a good hiking style. Be especially conscious about the following three things on the trail:

1. Hike at a sustainable pace

The JMT is an ultra ultra marathon, not a sprint. From an athletic point of view, this means that you need to keep your metabolism and energy conversion in an aerobic state. In brief, aerobic metabolism means that your muscles are receiving enough oxygen from your lungs, sufficient fuel through your bloodstream and have enough time to dispose of by-products from burning the fuel, especially lactic acid.

The aerobic state or respiration is usually the sweet spot for your body to process its energy – both from your nutritional intake as well as from fat storage. This allows you to access your long-term energy. Keep in mind that even very fit people have an average body fat level of 5-15 percent. That means that a 160lb/75kg person would have around

16lb/8kg of fat which contain approx. 56,000 calories – enough caloric energy for over 20 days. This body fat is a valuable reserve you should tap on the trail in order to keep your packed food weight low and potentially reduce your body weight as a pleasant side effect. Keeping a sustainable pace allows you to do just that. Additionally, your sustainable pace will reduce muscle fatigue and soreness because it allows your body to process and remove lactic acids as they build up during exercise.

Your personal sustainable pace will vary depending on your level of fitness, the altitude, heat, and time of day. However, variation should usually not be more than approx. +/- 20% of your average, unless there is an extra ordinarily difficult/steep section. Finding your personal sustainable pace is simple: it is the pace, at which you breathe deeply, but not rushed; you may sweat, but never excessively; and you do not feel the need to take a break before an hour or longer. Not taking a break but maintaining a steady pace is essential to keeping your metabolism up and you on your feet longer.

Remember, your personal sustainable pace is personal. It can be faster in the morning when it is still cool and slower at a sun-beaten incline. Don't be shy to keep a slow "step - one Mississippi - step" rhythm – important is merely that you feel you could hike this way for hours and days. In the end, a slow but sustainable pace will be fastest, because you will feel less fatigue and need less rest/recovery time.

2. Take small steps

In line with maintaining a sustainable pace, small steps avoid stress peaks for your muscles, reduce force of impact on your joints, and reduce the likelihood of a misstep injury. The JMT has varying trail conditions – at times you have well placed (but often tall) steps, other times you are walking over a little marked land slide field. You always have the option of leaping / taking a large step or you can instead place 2-3 steps, using slanted parts in front of a step to gain height or pick a closer rock to step on. Taking small, conscious steps keeps the strain on your muscles at a low level, avoiding muscle ache. Especially when hiking uphill with a full pack, small steps will reduce exhaustion and extend your range. Oppositely, descending with a full pack causes many to suffer from knee and ankle pain. The larger the step, the greater the vertical drop and hence impact to your joints. Lastly, small steps are less likely to go wrong. A small step has less momentum that could potentially cause you to twist your ankle or slip on loose gravel. With infrequent access to the JMT, avoiding any injury is the best way to go.

3. Always place your feet in the direction of the slope of the trail

The last recommendation is especially important when hiking downhill. Look at the direction and angle of the slope. Always place your foot so that it is in-line with the direction of the slope of the trail. If the path is going straight down the mountain, your toes should also point straight down. If there are switchbacks, you should adhere to the respective slope of the trail

Why? Think of it this way: if you do slip, you want your toes to shoot up/forward. You may land on your four letters or your backpack – but both are usually padded. If you had your foot at an angle to the slope and slipped, your body weight would follow the slope and push forward, twisting your ankle and potentially causing a painful injury at an inconvenient location. So remember: always point your toes to the slope.

Trekking Poles

Various forums and literature state that the use of trekking poles may increase your daily distance by up to 25%. Whether or not this is true, they have some definite advantages. When carrying a heavy pack, especially one in which the weight is not evenly distributed, you can easily lose your balance. Having poles secure in the ground gives quick relief. On the JMT you will also cross several rivers and streams – some on narrow logs, others on stepping stones. Your poles are especially handy here when a side step is quite inconvenient. When descending, trekking poles can be used to slow down your forward movement and unburden your knees. However: make sure to not overly strain your shoulders while relieving your knees.

The propulsion aspect of the trekking poles is also important. Though your legs will undoubtedly be doing most of the work, your upper body can support them. Make sure that your poles are adjusted to the right length. This should be approx. 0.7 x your height. Securely fasten your poles after adjustment. Then, when taking a stride with the left leg, set your right pole in front of your right, rear foot (Figure 7, 3). In this position, smoothly but forcefully push back. Then, gently lift the right pole tip slightly above the ground as you bring the left pole forward. Place the left pole in front of your left, rear foot (Figure 7, 5). Engage and repeat.

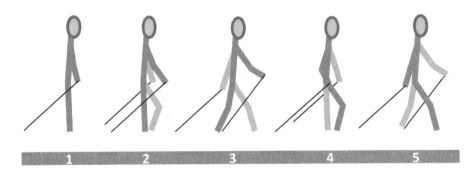

Figure 7 Trekking Poles Use

Be sure not to ram the poles into the ground. This causes stress on your wrists and shoulders and leads to earlier exhaustion. Also, you seldomly want your energy to go straight into the ground, but rather into a forward movement. Note how in Figure 7 the poles are never vertical, but always at an angle so that you push forward and not down. If you do decide to use trekking poles on the JMT, make sure to familiarize yourself with the right technique. When used incorrectly, hiking poles can cause pain and injuries to shoulders and wrists.

Adjust the straps so that they fit snugly around your wrists. This way, your wrist receives an even force from the top and your hands do not need to grip tightly at all. Only when you lift the pole from its most rear position, firm your grip with pinky and ring finger to elevate the pole's tip from the ground.

Allow yourself phases of rest from applying your trekking poles. Hold them in their balanced-middle while hiking along flat, easy stretches of the JMT with your shoulders either dangling down loosely or keeping your natural walking stride motion without the poles striking the ground.

Before taking poles on the JMT it is very useful to try them on a nearby trail to see how they feel. Practice the motion which is a little different from your usual one. If you cannot get comfortable or find that poles cause additional exhaustion, let it be. Especially if you already have problems with your shoulders or wrists, poles may cause unnecessary stress.

Additionally, exercises with light to medium weights are great to strengthen shoulder and back muscles that will be needed for pole use. A good exercise can be done with dumb bells of 5-25lb/2-12kg, called "90 degree dumbbell lateral raise".

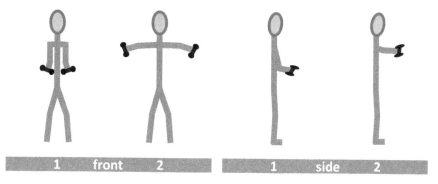

Figure 8 Shoulder Exercise for Trekking Pole Use

Stand with your feet at shoulder's width, your back slightly slanted forward and your core muscles engaged. Start by holding the weights in your hands with your elbows in a 90° angle touching your ribs and under arms extended straight in front of your body. In a slow, smooth motion, raise elbows from your ribs to shoulder's height. Hold briefly and return into the starting position. Choose a weight that allows you to repeat at least 3 sets of 15-20. Remember to flex both your abdominal as well as your lower back muscles to support a sturdy stance.

c. Food

This will be the most important chapter to some. And food should not be underestimated in its ability to revive energy and keep spirits up. Looking forward to a good meal is motivational and having it in your tummy lets you fall asleep satisfied. Putting effort into planning and preparing balanced meals with a lot of variety is well worth it. Nothing is worse than knowing you will have to eat something you do not want to.

Here are some guidelines for choosing your food:

- Weight: your food should be as dry and light as possible (incl. packaging)
- Nutritional value: combine foods to ensure an adequate supply of vitamins and minerals
- Caloric distribution: balance approx. 15% protein, 60% carbohydrates, and 25% fat per meal
- Non-perishable: your food must not spoil for two weeks or longer at up to 90°F/30°C
- Easy preparation: save gas, time, dirty pots, and nerves after a long day

Determining how much food to bring has two aspects. Firstly, it is a matter of calories. Your meals should provide approx. 1.5-2 times the calories you usually consume per day. Calculate higher calories when in low temperatures vice versa. Additional hunger can be satisfied with snacks. Secondly, it is a question of space. If you are planning to do the JMT in 22 days with just one drop off, you will have to be extremely conscious of what to bring, as it must all fit into a park approved bear proof canister. The largest single canisters store approx. 3gal/12ltr and weigh around 2lb/1kg. Using a second canister means a significant increase of dead weight and space throughout your journey. Dealing with these restrictions on space usually outdoes weight issues – the less space you have the less water and air content should be in your food packaging. This makes for a dense nutritional value. Generally, you should aim for about 1-2lb/ ½-1kg per person per day.

Either way, you will most likely face space issues in your canister. It helps to repackage your food into single servings (zip lock bags work well, can be labeled and reused for tissue paper), drain any air, and cut off excess packaging. As you stuff the canister, try to make layers of meals per day, rather than locking in all breakfasts at the bottom, etc. This makes accessing your food more convenient. Furthermore, stack the most perishable food items at the top of your canister for early consumption.

After preparing food at camp, do dishes at least 100ft/30m from your campsite. Likewise, be sure to pack any leftovers and store your bear canister at least 100ft/30m away, preferably in a shaded spot downwind of camp. Never store the bear canister or other scented items in your tent!

In addition to your main meals (if you choose so), good snacks can provide valuable nourishment as well. Supplements such as multi vitamin / multi mineral, magnesium, calcium, etc. can fill the last gap. If you are on a low sodium diet, ask your doctor if a higher sodium intake on the trail due to perspiration would be appropriate or not.

The following two pages provide some suggestions on which type of food to bring along:

Breakfast

- Instant oatmeal (purchase with or add flavors and sugar), porridge, semolina, and polenta with dried fruits
- Self-mixed cereals - with sesame, chia, flax, sunflower, pumpkin and other seeds; raisins and other dried fruit and berries; nuts; coconut flakes; rolled oats, shredded wheat, multi grains, etc.; mixed with dry milk, powdered soy, coconut, or almond milk, and possibly protein powder
- Pumpernickel (dark rye bread), tortilla, pita, or other dense, long-lasting breads
- Almond and peanut butter; tahini (sesame paste); chocolate spread; jelly and honey
- Freeze dried breakfasts such as scrambled egg, hash brown, or other
- Tea bags, tea pouches (such as ginger granulate), coffee, hot chocolate, sugar

Lunch

- Canned meat, smoked/dried sausage (e.g. traditional salami), beef and other jerkeys
- Tuna and salmon in pouches; canned fish and mussels in sauces; dried salted fish and shrimp
- Hard boiled eggs (early trail days)
- Powdered hummus (add water and olive oil)
- Crackers (wheat, whole grain, quinoa, corn); breads and tortillas
- Vegemite, pouches of olive oil and herbs; other veggie/vegan spreads
- Aged cheeses - repackaged in breathable material keep rather well

Snacks

- Almonds, pistachios, other nuts and seeds (with/out flavors, smoked, no shells)
- Dried fruits (mango, apricot, banana, date, fig, apple, etc.) and berries; fruit leather
- Power bars and gels; protein, granola, and cereal bars; other candy and snack bars
- Sundried tomatoes, veggie chips, olives in oil
- Dried corn kernels for popcorn in the evening (refine with oil, salt, sugar)
- Chocolate, gummy bears, caramel bonbons (limit these "empty calories")

Dinner

- Freeze dried instant meals in pouches (try different varieties, flavors, and brands prior)
- Pasta with sundried tomatoes, tomato paste, and/or pesto, olive oil and spices, parmesan
- Quinoa, millet, and couscous with herbs and spices (and dried carrots, onion, peas)
- Soup base or stock cubes, add noodles or rice and flakes of mushroom, parsley, tomato, etc.
- Ramin noodles and other instant dishes (e.g. macaroni & cheese, dried mashed potatoes)
- Burritos with rice, chicken in a pouch, beans, cheese, dried bell pepper
- Mixed lentils, beans, and chickpeas with seasoning (mind the cooking times)
- Condiments: salt, spices, little sachets of mustard, ketchup, hot sauce, soy sauce, olive oil
- Herbal tea, instant hot chocolate, hot lemon with honey

As you plan your meals, mind the respective cooking times and utensils needed for preparation. Anything that requires boiling for over 10min can be bothersome. Similarly, at camp preparations such as cutting/peeling/mashing or meals that require a lot of attention and flipping with spatulas can be a hassle to the exhausted or impatient. Many plan their meals so that their only kitchen gear is a small gas stove, one pot and one spoon. Nevertheless, whatever meals you decide to go with, bring along adequate equipment and know your own patience.

Despite the suggestions given above, some will choose not to prepare meals at all. We met a 64-year-old on the trail who ate nothing but power bars. He said he was quite content and did not get sick of them in his 15(!) trail days. Others eat a quick cereal bar for breakfast, pack- and warm-up while getting going, thus saving time and gas for a hot breakfast. Some alternate their food strategy depending on the campsite, the arrival time, and the difficulty of the day ahead – nice spots and slow days might invite you to enjoy a nice morning coffee or spend a long evening with celebratory dining. In summary, your food strategy is a matter of your personal preference, the tightness of your schedule, access to food / your resupply strategy, and access to gas.

d. Resupply

All but extreme hikers will need at least one resupply on the JMT. Commonly, bear canisters hold 6-10 days of food, depending on how much food you calculate, and how well you package, compress and pack it. So if your itinerary exceeds the restrictions of the bear canister, sending yourself food and goods to a pick-up destination is a simple remedy.

You have three options for your resupply: to send yourself a package to a cabin, to a post office, or to have your resupply dropped off close to you - see the list below. Post offices are cheapest, but quite far off and have limited office hours. Scheduled drop-offs are the most convenient, but also most expensive and inflexible. Cabins have the advantage that they often offer other food and hiking gear for sale (especially stove gas, which cannot be mailed), and sometimes have other amenities like a restaurant or showers. Also, some cabins have cache bins where hikers drop excess food, swap, or stock up on things. You usually find essentials like rice, cereal, and nuts, but also sunscreen and other goods in the bins. However, do not rely on using the cache and keep in mind the Pacific Crest Trail hikers traveling 2,665mi/4,288km from Mexico to Canada, who may depend on the left behind goodies.

As packaging for your resupply, you should choose a water tight and rodent resistant container. Do not use standard cardboard boxes as they may soak and/or be broken into by mice while your package awaits you in a remote mountain cabin. A proven container is a plastic bucket with lid from the hardware store (usually 5gal and around $5). The lid seals rather tightly, but should be securely taped down along with the handle. If you are using one bucket per person per resupply, remember that whatever does not fit in the bucket, will not fit in your bear canister. That leaves you with one day's worth of food and goodies that your resupply should maximally provide in excess of your bear canister's capacity.

But for this one day's worth of extra food, you can go all out. Apples and carrots keep well, and having something fresh will be one of your strongest cravings. Another one may be wine (in a carton, as you will not want to carry out a bottle), or other sweets and goodies. More practical content of your resupply should obviously be the planned meals and snacks for the remaining trip, toilet paper, sunscreen, vitamin & mineral supplements, blister treatment, bandages, and other things you might have used up by then. It helps to make a pack list of items and/or spread them out on the floor, grouping them in days and "extras" (e.g. sunscreen) to make sure you have everything and in the right quantities (see Appendix A).

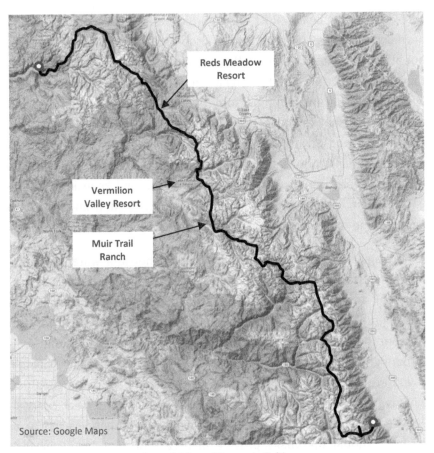

Reds Meadow
Resort

Vermilion
Valley Resort

Muir Trail
Ranch

Figure 9 Map of Resupply Cabins

Resupply Cabins

Reds Meadow Resort - www.redsmeadow.com

Reds Meadow Resort (RMR) is near the Devil's Postpile, a magnificent rock formation that lies opposite the JMT on the other side of the Middle Fork San Joaquin River. To get to RMR heading south, leave the JMT for 2.1mi/3.4km near soda springs and walk right past the Devil's Postpile or you can stay on the JMT and take the marked RMR junction cut-off.

Location: 60mi/97km from Happy Isles, Yosemite

Detour Length: Practically 0mi/km via Devil's Postpile and 0,6mi/1km round trip from RMR Jct

Price: $35 per bucket for mail in, $1 per day holding fee for self-drop-offs

Reds Meadow Resort			
Stove gas/fuel	Yes	Showers for hikers	Yes
Food and other gear for sale	Yes	Food cache	No
Restaurant for hikers	Yes	Lodging / camping	Yes

 There are hot springs and restrooms at the Reds Meadow Campground 0.7mi/1km north of RMR off of Reds Cir road. Soaking in warm water after a few trail days is incredible.

Vermilion Valley Resort - www.edisonlake.com

The Vermilion Valley Resort (VVR) is at the western tip of Lake Edison. Southbound hikers leave the JMT at Lake Edison Jct and either take the water taxi after 1.4mi/2.3km or continue to hike for 4.8mi/7.7km around the north shore. Northbound hikers exit the JMT at Bear Ridge Jct and walk approx. 7.8mi/12.6km along Bear Ridge Trail, across the dam, and along the shore.

Location: 88mi/142km from Happy Isles, Yosemite

Detour Length: approx. 9mi/14km – depends on routes taken

Price: $20 per bucket, 25lb max. Water taxi: $12 one way, $19 round trip

Vermilion Valley Resort			
Stove gas/fuel	Yes	Showers for hikers	Yes
Food and other gear for sale	Yes	Food cache	Yes
Restaurant for hikers	Yes	Lodging / camping	Yes

The water taxi usually runs from June 1 – October 1, depending on snow and water levels. Additionally, there is a shuttle for $10 to Bear Ridge or Bear Creek, by-passing inclines for southbound hikers leaving VVR.

 Hikers get their first beer for free as well as one night in a hiker's cabin or their tent site for free.

Muir Trail Ranch - www.muirtrailranch.com

Muir Trail Ranch (MTR) is located most centrally between Yosemite and Whitney, along the trail to Florence Lake via which its and your supplies are shipped. Southbound hikers exit the JMT at the North MTR / Sallie Keyes cut-off and descend for approx. 1mi/1.6km. Northbound hikers leave the JMT onto the South MTR cut-off towards Blayney Meadows and Florence Lake. MTR has 10+ large cache buckets.

Location: 106mi/170km from Happy Isles, Yosemite

Detour Length: 1mi/1.6km

Price: $65 per bucket, 25lb max., $2 per pound in excess

Muir Trail Ranch			
Stove gas/fuel	Yes	Showers for hikers	No
Food and other gear for sale	Yes	Food cache	Yes
Restaurant for hikers	No	Lodging / camping	Yes

There is a hot spring amidst high grass and bushes next to a crystal clear lake at the south edge of Shooting Star Meadow, just 0.6mi/1km south of MTR across the San Joaquin River. You should not miss this spot. Enter 37.234051,-118.88251 in an online map and ask for directions at MTR.

Post Offices

There are some scattered post offices in the vicinity of the JMT, but most cannot be easily reached. Somewhat accessible lays Mammoth Lakes Post Office at a detour of approx. 18mi/29km round trip from the JMT and approx. 60mi/96km from Happy Isles Yosemite. Should you decide to send yourself a package for general delivery, address it to:

[First & Last Name]

General Delivery

[Town], [State] [Zip Code] - 9999

HOLD UNTIL: [Date]

The zip code + "-9999" indicates general delivery. Packages will be held up to 30 days. Further information on post offices, office hours (!), etc. can be found at www.usps.com.

Resupply Delivery

For most JMT hikers, a resupply delivery or "dunnage drop" is not the most economical form of restocking food. The deliveries require a packer and one mule per 150lb of load; packers are approx. $220 per day, mules approx. $100 per day; and some trips require more than one day. Get in touch with the pack stations and inquire about the specifics in your time of travel.

These are the two most cited pack stations:

Rainbow Pack Outfitters, Located on the South Fork of Bishop Creek serving the John Muir Wilderness and Sequoia and Kings Canyon National Parks. Resupply delivery atop Bishop Pass or down to Le Conte Canyon, approx. 135mi/217km from Happy Isles Yosemite. www.rainbowpackoutfit.com, Phone: 760-873-8877.

Sequoia Kings Pack Train, Located west of Independence serving the John Muir Wilderness and Sequoia and Kings Canyon National Parks. The Sierra Nevada's oldest continuing pack outfit. Resupply services, showers and store. www.sequoiakingspacktrain.com, Summer phone: 800-962-0775, Winter phone: 760-387-2627.

For more pack stations see Appendix E [Resupply Delivery].

6. Gear

a. Clothing

"My face is sweating, but I'm still freezing." – This is a normal morning in the High Sierra. While the clear air and high altitudes allow the sun to shine with unknown power in early hours, they are also responsible for rapid temperature drops after sunset. So if you are hiking in the summer months, apart from a rare rain shower, days will be warm and nights will be cold. It's that simple.

Warm – 9:00am to 6:00pm

During the day, most hikers wear shorts or light hiking pants. Pants keep dust off your legs, which is a bit of an issue on the dry trails, and provide sun protection. Shorts are cooler and generally less restrictive. On this note, make sure your underwear does not rub and chafe your thighs, even when moist; biker shorts without padding can be a good option.

A (short-sleeve) t-shirt is sufficient temperature wise while you are in motion, but long sleeved and high collared shirts offer lotion-free sun protection. There are both light, classic-cut button shirts with folding collars as well as thin, long-sleeved t-shirts with high zipper collars.

 If possible, pick a shirt without seams on the shoulders to avoid rubbing and pressure points from your pack straps.

Most hikers also opt for some form of head dress – a brimmed hat, visor, base cap, cap with neck flap, or other. Given the warmth, any alternative should be vented well but provide good UV protection. South bound hikers will get more sun in their face, while northbound hikers receive more rays on their necks.

Cold – 6:00pm to 9:00am

As the sun disappears behind the surrounding peaks, you will quickly miss your mid-day nemesis. A good first warming layer is a light merino wool sweater or fleece jacket. When you have settled at camp, sitting and waiting for dinner, you will want to add another layer. Puffy down jackets offer great warmth for their weight and compress well; puffy synthetic jackets are a cost effective alternative. And to be prepared, you should also bring one light outer shell rain jacket / wind breaker.

If you decided to walk in shorts during the day, it is still advisable to bring long pants for the evenings, especially when in company - otherwise, you can use long johns. Then, in your sleeping bag, long underwear bottoms and long sleeved tops are best suited to keep your sleeping bag clean and yourself warm. If you choose comfortable long-sleeve t-shirts for hiking, a clean one works well for sleeping, too.

Useful accessories for the cold are a fleece or knitted beanie, and/or a multi-functional headwear (acts as scarf, hat, headband, etc.) to keep your head warm at camp. Gloves for packing up and grasping your trekking poles in the morning are very nice to have, but not a must.

For example, this was my clothing pack list:

2 hiking socks (pairs)	1 t-shirt
2 underwear	1 fleece jacket
1 long underwear	1 warm (!) puffy jacket
1 shorts	1 rain shell
1 hiking pants	1 visor
1 long sleeved t-shirt (with high zip collar)	1 beanie

 For all of your clothing, try to avoid cotton.

There are many light, moisture wicking, fast drying, stretchy, and comfortable materials out there today that are far superior to cotton. Also, clothes with less pockets and zippers will dry faster and are less likely to damage one another during washing. Since water is abundant and the air is dry, you can wash your clothes every day, they will dry fast, and you do not need to pack much.

As an intermediate item between clothing and hiking, you may want to consider bringing flip-flops, sandals, or other light foot-wear. Arriving at camp and knowing you can take your shoes off becomes ever more appealing with each mile traveled. Opt for a light weight solution with little capabilities other than keeping your bare feet off the jagged rocks.

b. Hiking

Shoes & Boots

Undoubtedly the most stressed piece of gear on your trip will be your shoes. Any good shoe has a thick, cushioning sole with non-slip tread. Beyond that, there are different opinions on which style is best suited – hiking boot, hiking shoe, or trail runner. An estimated 30 percent of JMT hikers wear boots, while 70 percent opt for a sub-ankle shoe[9].

Hiking Boot   Hiking Shoe   Trail Runner

Figure 10 Hiking Shoes & Boots[10]

---

[9] Estimate, own observation.
[10] Sketches of Asolo boot and Salomon shoes

Hiking boots provide more stability to the ankles. A well-fitting boot is snug, supports the ankle and reduces the risk of twisting on a slight misstep. With more contact area, the foot can be less likely to move back and forth in a good boot. The high rising sides also offer ankle protection from hitting rocks and prevent sand/dust from entering the boot. Other advantages of a boot are warmth and water resistance, however, neither is relevant for the JMT. Drawbacks of boots are greater weight, stiffness (and hence resistance during walking strides), chances of blisters from ill-fitting boots, and lower breathability.

Hiking shoes combine the grip stability of a good boot with more flexibility. The low cut allows more mobility and light mesh uppers enable moisture wicking. Watch out for firm heel support and a plastic cap to protect your toes. Different brands have various lacing systems; some enable great fit in minimal time. Hiking shoes are lighter than boots and generally feel less restrictive while still providing sufficiently firm stability. Drawbacks are reduced ankle support and incompatibility with crampons (irrelevant for JMT in the summer).

Trail runners go one step further regarding agility and lightness, weighing about as much as a running shoe. In order to save that weight, trail runners usually provide less cushioning than hiking shoes, while still offering good tread and lots of grip. Upper materials are mostly breathable, light meshes – offering more support than running shoes but far less than a boot; quick lacing systems are also available. Generally, trail runners are aimed at people going for a run in the mountains or woods, not necessarily long hiking trips with heavy backpacks. Drawbacks are low overall support and cushioning.

Whichever shoe or boot you decide to go with, make sure you are confident about your choice. It should provide adequate support to you and your pack weight, wick moisture from your feet, not be too heavy and tiring, have a well cushioned sole and, most importantly, a padded inside that does not cause blisters. Get at least half a size bigger than you normally would so that you can wear padded socks and to prevent your toes from hitting against the tips when descending. The shoe does not have to be especially water resistant, as neither rain, wet crossings, nor snow is an issue.

I strongly recommend using your prospective shoes on a few hikes to break them in and see how they handle. If in doubt, try another pair – getting your shoes right is essential. Then again, do not take shoes that are too worn down and have little tread left. You would not want their early exodus on the 222 miles.

Socks & Gaiters

A good sock can significantly add to your hiking comfort. Most modern trail socks are made of merino wool or polyester. Both fibers have outstanding properties regarding moisture wicking and temperature regulation. Thick socks, especially those with hidden seams, provide cushioning and help the shoe evenly embrace your foot, reducing rubbing and blisters. Though less stylish in a shoes-shorts combo and slightly warmer, socks that go (well) above your ankle collect less sand and stones, keep your legs cleaner, and protect against the sun.

Another way to keep out sand and stones are gaiters. Besides high gaiters for snow treks, there are also short and light ones, specifically designed for hikers wearing shorts and low socks. The gaiters wrap around above your ankle and go over your shoes, protecting the gap between sock and shoe from unwanted entrants.

Compression socks can be of use especially to those who have issues with blood clots, edema, and thrombosis. Compression socks come in different lengths, from knee- and thigh-high, to full pantyhose style. There are different compression gradients to assist circulation; lower ones are usually prescription free while higher compressions may require consultation. In either case, if you are aware of a condition and/or over 40, it might be wise to get your doctor's opinion.

Backpacks

Just like shoes, an ill-fitting backpack can cause considerable pain – chaffing along straps or back aches from a restrictive fit. There is also a multitude of styles, capacities, and functionalities. Here is a list of decision criteria to find a pack that is right for you:

Criteria	Comment
Size	<table><tr><th>Size</th><th>Torso [inch]</th><th>Torso [cm]</th></tr><tr><td>Extra Small</td><td>up to 15 ½</td><td>up to 40</td></tr><tr><td>Small</td><td>15 ½ - 17½</td><td>40 - 45</td></tr><tr><td>Medium</td><td>17½ - 19½</td><td>45 - 50</td></tr><tr><td>Large</td><td>19½ and up</td><td>50 and up</td></tr></table> These are commonly used sizes. Learn how to measure your torso on page 57. Some packs also come in different hip sizes; measure at widest part. Apart from the (vertical) torso size, the design and cut varies on packs and shoulder straps, making them more or less comfortable for broad or narrow shouldered people, etc. Compare and try different packs.
Capacity	Typical packs used on the JMT have capacities of 65-80 ltr. All packing capacity is measured in liters and for the medium size – small and large can vary by -/+ 3ltr. While you want to choose the smallest capacity to save weight, you also need to fit all your gear. The right capacity for you depends on how bulky your big items are, i.e. tent, sleeping bag, and pad, and how much and which clothing you plan to bring. Packs allow some flexibility by raising the top lid or strapping a tent or foam pad on the outside. However, this may mean that weights are not optimally distributed (see Chapter 6 *Pack & Adjust*). Also keep in mind that your bear canister will take up a significant portion of your pack.

Weight	As with most other gear, the weight of a backpack is closely linked to comfort and price. Thick, comfortable padding along shoulder straps and hip belts add to the scale. However, investing "weight" in comfort here can pay out, since you will be carrying this pack all day for over two weeks. Besides padding, the durability of materials affects the pack's weight. Light packs usually have very thin shell materials. If you are not at all cautious about where and how you set down your pack each time you take a break, this could be a problem. Lighter packs may also be less water resistant. However, for the JMT, this is not a decision criterion.
Padding	Mentioned as an aspect of weight and ventilation, the padding of the shoulder straps, the hip belt, and along the back of the pack is the essential factor for how you perceive the comfort of a pack – especially when filled with over 44lb/20kg. Ultra-light packs save weight here; make sure you are comfortable with the limited padding and that there is no rubbing/chaffing when the pack is loaded and you are in normal hiking motion.
Adjustability	Most modern internal frame packs are very similar regarding their adjustability. Shoulder straps and hip belts can be adjusted in length; load lifter straps connect the pack's top to the shoulder straps and keep the weight balanced near your center; sternum straps connect the shoulder straps across the chest to snug the pack's fit and increase stability. Some packs have an adjustable suspension, meaning the entire shoulder harness system can be slid up and down to customize the pack to the exact torso length. On the other side of the backpack, compression straps along the sides and front of the pack pull the weight

	close to your center and keep contents from shifting on difficult trails; daisy chains[11], elastic straps, or tool loops allow you to arrange and adjust gear on the outside of the pack.
Compartments	Having certain compartments may not be a key decision factor, however, having a well though-out design can make trail days easier. Some hikers may insist on a sleeping bag compartment at the bottom of the pack; others may look for a minimum amount of side pockets to organize and access their content; others may want one or two water bottle pockets, if this is their chosen hydration strategy. A multitude of compartments may, however, conflict with a minimalist, ultra-light approach.
Ventilation	A well-ventilated back area with airy padding is a big plus – especially on the JMT. Keep ventilation in mind when choosing a pack. It not only adds to your general comfort but a dry back and shoulders are also less susceptive to chaffing. Different brands and models have various approaches at how to wick moisture and heat from in-between your back and your pack. Some have air channels between padding; others completely separate the pack from the hiker's back with a tension mesh. Some ventilation methods are more effective and/or comfortable than others. Try them out; there is no rating for comparison.
Hydration	A standard feature on most packs and worth asking about: a clip inside the pack to hang the hydration pack and an opening to lead the drinking tube to the front.

---

[11] daisy chain: row of vertical loops of webbing, commonly placed up along the center of the pack

Frame	There are two frame styles: internal and external frames. Most modern packs have frames sewed (internally) into the bag. Packs formerly only had external frames, with large aluminum tubes extending above and around the pack. Advantages of the external frame packs are low cost, light weight, and easy packability of bulky items (esp. on the outside). Disadvantages are their limited adjustability and fit, they are less stable on uneven terrain, and they are usually less water resistant. Internal packs make up for the above disadvantages, but are usually more expensive, esp. when weight is considered.
Rain cover	A built-in rain cover, usually located in the top lid or at the bottom of the pack, can be wrapped around the entire backpack with an elastic trimming. They are very practical, but not crucial on the JMT. Also, they can be substituted with a plastic trash bag and a bit of tape in the rare occasion of demand.

Table 4 Backpack Decision Criteria

Excurse: Measuring your torso length:

1. Locate your 7th cervical vertebra (C7) at the base of your neck by tilting your head forward. It is the bony bump at the end your vertical spine as your neck is leaning forward. When you run your fingers down your neck, you will first feel the smaller C6 and then C7. This marks the top of your torso.
2. Locate your iliac crest at the top of your hip bone by placing your hands high on your hips. With your thumbs in the back, dig into your pelvis to find the rounded, highest point of your hip bone. The imaginary line between your thumbs marks the bottom of your torso.
3. Measure between top and bottom of your torso. Be sure to stand straight. Assistance while handling the tape measure is helpful.

Trekking Poles

Chapter 5 *Preparation & Planning* offered some advice on how to correctly use trekking poles. They can be of great service both for propulsion and providing a sense of security on steep stretches of trail. Here is what to look out for when purchasing trekking poles:

- Good fit of grip and wrist strap: avoid sweaty grips (cork is good) and chafing straps.
- The length of the pole should be easily adjustable.
- The clipping / screwing adjustment mechanism, as well as the overall pole, should be sturdy.
- The lighter the pole, the better. Light weight assists the correct use and is less exhausting.
- Shock absorbers can be useful, but are mostly a matter of taste. Try them out.
- Rubber tips absorb shock and muffle impact noise. More grip on rock, less on soft subsoil

c. Sleeping

This section supports your decisions in putting together a comfortable sleeping environment. To most, this will consist of a tent, sleeping bag, and a pad. However, there are some alternatives.

Shelters

If you are hiking as a couple, you will probably share a tent. Should you be joined by a hiking buddy, the weight savings might be exceeded by the benefits of separate sleeping arrangements. Here, you have three options to choose from:

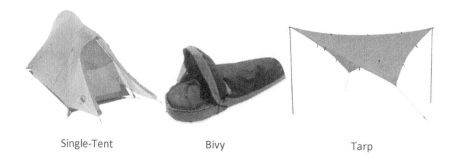

| Single-Tent | Bivy | Tarp |

Figure 11 Sleeping Shelter Options[12]

Tent

A tent provides the most space for you to dress and move around inside as well as for keeping your gear sheltered. Remember, not only rain but also condensation – especially in close proximity to lakes and rivers – will settle overnight and can soak your gear. If it does happen to rain, is very windy, and/or you are cold, quickly pitching your tent and jumping inside is comforting; and getting food ready while taking a look at the map inside can be quite cozy. While the lightest single person tents are only around 2lb/1kg, carrying a tent is the heaviest option for shelter. Also, because tent fabric is so thin in order to save weight, adding a footprint (a sheet that is placed underneath the tent) is a useful addition. The footprint protects against moisture and punctures from underneath, but adds some weight to the setup.

Bivy

A bivy (also bivouac sack) is slightly bigger than a sleeping bag. The sleeping bag slides into the bivy, which is made of water and wind resistant material. A bivy bag has a small hole or breathable fabric in the head area and is either left open or zipped shut. A bivy shelter has a little dome in the head area, giving some space to rest on your elbows inside. While bivys offer similar insulation and protection from the

---

[12] Tent: Big Agnes, Bivy: Outdoor Research, Tarp: Kelty

elements as tents, inner condensation is a greater problem, because it gets in direct contact with the sleeping bag and has less air circulation. Also, bivys offer no additional space for gear or greater movement and people with claustrophobia may fear the confined space.

Under the Stars / Tarp

To anyone counting ounces, a tent or even bivy might sound like tons. An alternative widely discussed in forums is sleeping under the stars, as the night sky is spectacular. And reiterating the saying, "it never rains at night in the Sierra", you have a very good chance of waking up dry. That is, as long as you have been diligent in selecting your campsite. In case of a nightly surprise or for shelter during the day, a simple tarp that is tied at 3-4 corners is a minimalist's reply to the elements. However, tarps will rarely be as good a wind deflector or as insulating as a tent or bivy. So when choosing this alternative, make sure your sleeping bag is adequate to combat the temperatures including the wind-chill. Obviously, a simple tarp is the lightest and cheapest shelter, but offers the least protection and privacy.

On the JMT, I used a single person tent with footprint and was very content with my decision. My sleeping bag/pad combo was not adequate at all (see Chapter 7a *Plan*) so I was grateful for the shelter. As an additional insulation, I spread a silver emergency blanket beneath my pad to block the ground's creeping cold. I appreciated being able to keep my belongings under the vestibule[13] and un-/packing in a dirt free environment inside. I enjoyed an evening routine of moving inside the tent, changing, applying a balm to my ankles and knees, hanging my light inside my tent, reviewing the map and comparing actual to planned distances travelled, taking short diary notes, and finally preparing for the next day.

---

[13] Vestibule: the staked-out front extension of a tent's rainfly that forms a sheltered area.

Sleeping Bags

Sleeping bags come in an overwhelming multitude of varieties. It is all the more important to understand which are the relevant features for this adventure and those to come. A sleeping bag is a significant investment that should last for 15+ years.

Warmth, expressed by the bag's temperature rating, is your primary decision factor. Fortunately, there is an EN Standard[14] warmth measurement that lets you easily compare. Depending on which month you are planning for, choose a bag with a comfort zone temperature that is equal to or lower than the average low temperature of that month. For example, average daily lows on the JMT in summer drop to around 40°F/4°C, so your sleeping bag should have a comfort zone of 40°F/4°C, 35°F/2°C, or lower to be on the safe side. Appropriate comfort zones for the JMT are usually found among 3-season sleeping bags.

All peak performance sleeping bags use down insulation with fill-powers[15] of 700-900. Down is breathable and provides incredible loft and resulting insolation for its light weight while also compressing well. Additionally, there are new hydrophobic/dry downs that maintain insulation properties after getting wet and/or repel moisture. Modern synthetic fill materials mimic the great properties of down, often at a very competitive price.

Weight is a general concern. Besides the filling, the weight is a function of length, girth, cut, fabric, and features of the bag. Length of the bag is usually a pretty clear decision based on your height. Girth will primarily be determined by our shoulders and belly or hips. Cut refers to the bag's shape: most bags available today are mummy style that follows the contours of the body – wider at the shoulders and narrow along legs and feet. Some bags are cut straight, providing more space but also more

---

[14] EN Standard 13537: a European Standard for the testing, rating, and labelling of sleeping bags.
[15] Fill-power: a measure of loft in cubic inch; it describes to what volume one ounce of down expands to.

material to carry. Fabrics lining the sleeping bag are usually made of lightweight synthetic materials. Features include, for instance, hoodies, draft tubes[16], zippers, and inside pockets. Take a look at different features and styles and see if you are passionate about any of them. If not, cross them off your list of "must-have" for your sleeping bag and save the weight.

Combining the above leads to the warmth-to-weight ratio. This figure compares the bag's temperature rating to its weight. Best ratios are achieved with hood-less, no-frills, down mummy bags that have reduced padding in the back. However, going ultra-light requires some experience, especially on how to substitute certain savings on one piece of gear with another (but only if it is another part of your essentials; if it comes on top, it defeats the purpose). With sleeping bags, for instance, a lack of an attached hood can be compensated with a hooded down jacket and/or a warm hat, which anyone will most likely pack either way. The padding in the back, which is compressed when lying on it and hence loses its insulating properties, can be reduced if the pad offers sufficient insulation and when the hiker has a habit of lying flat on that side.

Pack size is another important factor. It is strongly correlated with the bag's warmth and weight - unfortunately also with its price. Everything that reduces the weight usually reduces the pack size. Oppositely, warmer bags with more filling typically do not compress as much. In this trade-off, do not opt for an inadequate comfort zone to reduce compression size unless you have a plan to make up for that loss of warmth.

Fit and feel should be agreeable - essentially, you need to be comfortable. The materials should feel pleasant and you should have sufficient space around your shoulders, hips, and feet. However, sufficient space is very subjective. Some find mummy sleeping bags to

---

[16] Draft tube: an insulating flap or tube that covers the zipper to avoid heat loss out of the sleeping bag.

be confining, some feel like suffocating with a draft collar, others like being snug. A good outdoor store should have several models for testing – try them and find out which type you are.

Lastly, choosing your sleeping bag must match your choice of camping strategy.

 If you are sleeping without a shelter, your sleeping bag should be especially warm, wind and water resistant.

However, water resistant shells are less breathable and require more time for your bag to loft. If you are planning to save weight on filling and frills and wearing your down jacket, make sure the sleeping bag provides enough inner space for the jacket's loft. In the end, deciding on one bag will be a compromise between all the contending traits and staying within a reasonable budget.

Sleeping Pads

A sleeping pad should literally support a good night's sleep. The two main criteria are cushioning and insulation. You can count on the ground being hard and cold wherever you camp along the JMT. There are three popular and equally suitable alternatives:

Air pads, similar to the ones used in swimming pools, have a thin air-tight shell that is inflated through a mouth valve. In order to cut down on weight, they are often semi-rectangular in shape. They are very light weight, roll-up very small, and offer exceptional cushioning - especially those with a thickness of 2in/5cm and up. On the downside, inflating a thick pad may require more than a minute of lung blasting, light weight models can be noisy due to crackling material, and punctures are a concern.

Foam pads are usually made of dense, closed-cell foams. They can either be rolled up or folded like an accordion. Foam pads are light, inexpensive, provide great insulation, and are practically indestructible from rough surfaces. On the downside, foam pads are usually not very thick and provide limited cushioning comfort. They also do not compress, hence packing rather large.

Self-inflating foam pads combine the pack-ability of an air pad with the cushioning of a foam pad, while needing only little additional inflation. Thin pads are light and well compressible into a small sack. On the downside, they offer limited cushioning, while thicker pads of over 2in/5cm are too heavy.

However you decide, make sure the pad is long enough and sufficiently wide at your shoulders. A good test is placing the pad on a hardwood floor or tiles and giving it a trial night.

Sleeping Gear

Apart from the clothing you wear in your sleeping bag, additional gear for comfort is some form of pillow, eye mask, ear plugs, and insect repellent.

 An alternative to packing an inflatable pillow is using your sleeping bag's stuff sack as a casing and stuffing it loosely with clothes.

Eye masks can be helpful for the sensitive during a bright full moon. Ear plugs are tricky – if you cannot catch any sleep due to surrounding noises, they are useful. Otherwise, it is surely favorable to be aware of rodents or even bears in the vicinity. Insect repellent can come in handy, especially when camping near water and in an open or without shelter.

Lighting in the dark is also important to think about – for camp preparations in the evenings, early or late hiking, reading in the tent, and when nature calls at night. Headlamps are great because you have both hands free, useful in any of the above scenarios; ensure adequate battery life. Solar lamps come in an increasing variety. You can be sure to get enough sun during the day to charge your device for another night. Either way, opt for energy efficient LED light sources and remember to keep your light handy at night.

d. Food & Drinks

While Chapter 5c *Food* discussed the type of food and drinks to bring and send as resupply, this Chapter focusses on the various gears needed to store, prepare, and eat the food as well as treat and store water.

Bear Canisters

For the storage of food and any other scented items, bear canisters are mandated in most stretches along the JMT – especially at Yosemite and Mt. Whitney. This means, you will carry a bear canister throughout your journey. As you may not need a bear canister on many other occasions, you can choose to rent, buy used, or buy new.

Bear canisters for rent are available at selected outdoor stores in California, directly from some manufacturers (see list below, Bearikade), and at most wilderness permit offices. Check the respective rental terms, especially regarding returning the canister via mail. Most permit offices for instance, demand in-person returns – except Yosemite. Any canisters for rent will usually be approved models, but ask just in case. The most common rental model is the Garcia, used by the permit offices.

When purchasing a new bear canister, there are a few things to look out for. As a first step, the canister must be national park approved (SIBBG for black bears, IGBC for grizzly bears).

Here is a list of the currently approved models:

- Backpacker Model 812 (Garcia), www.backpackerscache.com
- BearVault 110b, 200, 250, 300, 350, 400, 450, and 500, www.bearvault.com

- Bearikade Weekender and Expedition (both 1766 and higher), www.wild-ideas.net
- The Bear Keg (Counter Assault), www.counterassault.com
- The Bare Boxer Contender (101) and Champ (202), www.bareboxer.com
- Lighter1 Big Daddy and Little Sami, www.lighter1.com
- UDAP No-Fed-Bear, www.udap.com
- Purple Mountain Engineering Tahoe

Source: www.nps.gov/yose/planyourvisit/containers.htm

The most important criterion for choosing a canister is its size. Depending on your resupply strategy, you will want to get the smallest/lightest canister for the maximum amount of days you will be carrying food for. For example, if you plan 2 resupplies, one after 5 days, the other after 6 days, and your last resupply provides 8 days of food, your bear canister should hold up to 8 days of food (7 if you plan on picking up the resupply in the morning). Do a dry run and try fitting what you plan on sending yourself in the canister.

Apart from the size, the above listed canisters primarily vary in weight, transparency, closing mechanism, and price. Table 5 compares four of the approved models between 615-703 cu in. / 10-11.5 ltr. With very good preparation and packing, a canister of around 700 cu in. / 11.5 ltr can provide food storage for up to 9-10 days.

The Big Daddy and BV500 are both made of transparent polycarbonate, allowing you to see what is inside and where – a very convenient feature – and both have lids that do not require a tool / coin. The Big Daddy lid doubles as a pan, but an inner cross bar is needed for stability. The BV500 has a screw-on lid with a click-lock mechanism that requires some well-aimed pressure to open. Both the Garcia 812's and the Bearikade's lids are secured by two/three locks which require a coin or alike to open. The Garcia Cache 812 is simple and cost effective. The Bearikade canisters can be custom ordered in many sizes; they are handmade of carbon fiber composite material, making them the lightest but also most expensive canisters on the market.

	Lighter1 Big Daddy	BearVault BV500	Garcia Backpackers' Cache 812	Bearikade Custom 703
Total Weight	2 lb 11oz / 1.22kg	2 lb 9oz / 1.16kg	2 lb 12oz / 1.25kg	2 lb / 0.9kg
Interior Volume	650 cu in. / 10.5 ltr	700 cu in. / 11.5 ltr	615 cu in. / 10.1 ltr	703 cu in. / 11.5 ltr
Dimensions [diameter x height]	8.7 in. x 13 in. / 22.1cm x 33cm	8.7 in. x 12.7 in. / 22.1cm x 32.3cm	8.8 in. x 12 in. / 22.4cm x 30.5cm	9 in. x 11.25 in. / 22.9cm x 28.6cm
Housing Material	poly-carbonate	poly-carbonate	ABS polymer	carbon fiber
Transparent	yes	yes	no	no
Tool Free Access	yes	yes	no	no
Price [$], approx.	105	80	75	285

Table 5 Bear Canister Comparison[17]

For buying a used bear canister, your best bets are semi-/ annual used gear sales at outdoor stores and Craigslist[18]. Make sure the lid closes securely. Also, if you have purchased a new canister, the before mentioned website is an easy way to sell it again.

 Bear spray, pepper spray, and other deterrents are prohibited in several national parks and especially in Yosemite National Park.

Using a bear canister properly and keeping your campsite food and odor free is precaution enough. Save the weight of carrying a spray that could harm both you and the wildlife.

---

[17] Information taken from respective manufacturer's website
[18] www.craigslist.com

Stoves & Fuel

The preparation of your meals will undoubtedly require a stove, as campfires are prohibited above certain elevations (see Chapter 4c *Campsites*) and illegal all together during droughts. Two stove fuel types are most common and almost certainly in stock at resupply cabins: gas canisters and liquid fuel.

Canisters are filled with a pressurized gas mix of isobutane and propane. They have a self-sealing valve at the top and a thread. Stoves can be screwed directly onto the tops. The thread securely fastens the stove to the canister, using it as a stand. These stoves are extremely light (< 3oz/85g) and pack very small.

Figure 12 Canister Stoves: Top and Remote (Inverted) Mounted

Stoves can also be connected remotely. These remote stoves are placed on the ground and connected to the canister via fuel line. Consequently, the canister can be flipped on its head – referred to as an inverted canister. Inverting the canister allows operation in liquid feed mode. This way, gas does not (need to) vaporize inside the canister. By avoiding the need for vaporization the gas can be used at lower (sub-evaporation) temperatures and performance is upheld. Especially in cold conditions this comes in handy as the output is increased even with only little gas remaining. In addition, placing the stove directly on the ground can also improve pot stability and eases wind shielding.

The third pressurized gas setup is called an integrated canister system. These systems have an integrated burner and heat exchanger that are directly mounted to the bottom of a pot for optimum heat transfer. The compact units are well shielded against wind and their pots are often insulated against heat loss. Integrated canister systems are especially efficient for boiling water. However, it lies in their nature that they cannot be remotely fed and thus have limited cold weather performance.

Generally, all canister systems are easy and fast to use, as they do not require priming. They burn cleanly, reach their maximum heat very quickly, and there is no risk of fuel spillage. On the downside, the pressurized gas is rather expensive and gauging how much fuel is left is difficult. Upright mounted canisters (not inverted) have a risk of tipping over and struggle with the properties of gas, which lead to limited cold-weather operability and reduced performance as canisters empty.

Excurse: Operating pressurized gas canisters in cold weather - Understanding the limits

The lowest operating temperature of a pressurized gas canister is a matter of its gas composition. Good hiking canisters consist of isobutane and propane, large bbq canisters often contain n-butane. A canister gas' operating temperature limit is determined by the gas with the highest (warmest) boiling point. Since propane has the lowest boiling point temperature (see Table 6) it will burn off first, especially in an upright canister system.

Boiling Point	° Fahrenheit	° Celsius	Approx. Limit
N-Butane	31	+/- 0	41°F/5°C
Isobutane	12	-11	21°F/-6°C
Propane	-44	-42	-35/-37°C

Table 6 Boiling Points of Stove Canister Gases at Sea Level

If n-butane is left, the stove's working limit would be around 41°F/5°C, because the stove system needs a certain pressure to operate, which requires some thermal energy exceeding the respective boiling temperature to vaporize the gas. Otherwise, at lower temperatures, the n-butane would sit as a non-vaporizing liquid at the bottom of the canister. This explains the positive effect of a liquid-feed stove and inverting the canister. The composition of the liquid gases remain constant, i.e. the less cold weather adequate gas is not left behind to cause the canister to fade when approaching depletion.

A canister with a propane–isobutane mix would reach its limit around 21°F/-6°C. However, as the air pressure drops with increasing altitude, so do the gases' boiling points. So as you ascend, your gas canister will be able to operate at lower temperatures than at sea level. A lapse rate for this effect is to subtract 2°F from the temperature limit for every 1000ft in altitude gain or subtract 1°C for every 300m.

The excurse adds an important selection criterion: the gas composition. At the least for summer trips, canister stoves are very well suited for the JMT, if they contain a propane–isobutane mix. With an operating temperature limit of 21°F/-6°C at sea level and approx. 1°F/-16°C at 10,000ft/3,000m elevation, canister stoves will provide reliable heat along the trail. Liquid feed canister stoves offer additional low temperature range.

 Remember, the fuel temperature is key not the ambient temperature. When confronted with very cold conditions, keep your canister inside your tent or even at your feet in the sleeping bag to ensure the gas temperature is a few degrees above its boiling point.

Liquid fuel stoves have a similar setup to remote liquid-fed canister systems. The burner is placed on the ground and connects via fuel line to the bottle fuel tank, which has a pump to pressurize the fuel and a valve to control flow. Most systems require priming, especially in cold conditions. Priming means that a few drops of fuel are placed into a dish underneath the burner and lit. This heats the attached fuel line and causes the fuel to vaporize and press into the actual burner where it can be ignited.

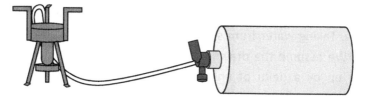

Figure 13 Liquid Fuel Stove

Liquid fuel systems are dominated by white gas (a.k.a. naphtha). This is a highly refined fuel with little impurities so it burns very clean. There are also multi-fuel stoves that run on white gas, kerosene, diesel, and gasoline. Generally, the greatest advantages of a (petroleum based) liquid fuel stove are the easy international availability of its fuels, their low cost, very high heat output, and their ability to operate at low temperatures. White gas, for example, freezes at −22°F/−30°C to which the stove is operable. Downsides are that some fuels are odorous, smoke, and may blacken pots; the stoves − esp. multi-fuel − are rather expensive; flames are not as finely adjustable for simmering foods; operation − incl. pumping and priming − needs some practice and bears risk of flare-ups or burns; and stoves require regular maintenance to avoid clogging − all the more, the less purified the fuel is. All this requires some experience and commitment.

Regarding weight, liquid fuel systems are heavier than canisters, due to the more complex burner and pump-valve system for the bottle tanks. Additionally, the commonly used pressurized gases have an approx. 5% higher energy density than the petroleum fuels. However, liquid fuel tanks are reusable and can be filled as needed, whereas gas canisters can only be bought in a few sizes, making incremental adjustments to fuel supplies difficult.

That leads to the very important question of how much fuel to carry. This is a function of how much mass needs to be heated from/to which temperature at which elevation, ambient temperature, and efficiency circumstances. Assuming we want 8oz/235ml of hot water for coffee in the morning and 8oz/235ml for porridge/oatmeal, none for lunch, and 16oz/470ml for an instant meal in the evening along with one cup of tea at 8oz/235ml, that adds up to 40oz/1.2ltr of boiling water per person per day. Taking water from steep side streams gives us clean, but cold water. We assume the drawn water comes at 50°F/10°C, but must be heated up by a delta of only 175°C/80°C, as water will boil around 195°F/90°C at 8200ft/2500m, which we assume as our average camp elevation.

With the specific heat capacity for water of 4.2 J·cm^3/K we calculate the energy to heat 40oz/1.2ltr from 50°F/10°C to 195°F/90°C:

$$Q_w = 4.2 \text{ J·cm}^3/\text{K} \times 80\text{K} \times 1200\text{cm}^3 = 403\text{kJ}$$

Assuming an average energy content for pressurized gas and petroleum fuels of approx. 19,000 BTU/lb or 44,200kJ/kg, we calculate the mass of fuel needed to provide above energy:

$$M_f = 403\text{kJ} / 44.2\text{kJ/g} = 9.12\text{g} \ (0.32\text{oz})$$

Now we would have our per day amount of fuel needed, if we were cooking in perfect conditions. However, not 100% of the burning fuel's energy goes into the water – significant parts are lost to the pot and the air. In order to account for these ambient and efficiency losses, we introduce a correction factor, assuming 1/3 of our fuel's energy is lost before our water boils.

$$M_{f\,corr} = 403\text{kJ} / 44.2 \text{ kJ/g} \times 1{,}5 = 13.68\text{g} \ (0.48\text{oz})$$

We now know that we need 0.48oz/13.68g of fuel per day to bring 40oz/1.2ltr of water to a boil. Consequently, one 8oz/227g canister of gas (gross weight 13.1oz/374g) would last for 16 days for one person. This is equal to an average fuel consumption of 11.5g fuel per liter or

0.37oz per 32oz. of water; therefore one 8oz/227g canister can boil approx. 5.4gal/20ltr of water. Integrated canister systems can achieve up to 20% better values.

! If you plan on simmering your food after the water has boiled, add 0.035oz/1g per minute of cooking time.

Figure 14 shows the equation with which to estimate fuel consumption per section. Remember to then consider all your sections and think about which fuel tank sizes or gas cartridges are best suited to minimize weight.

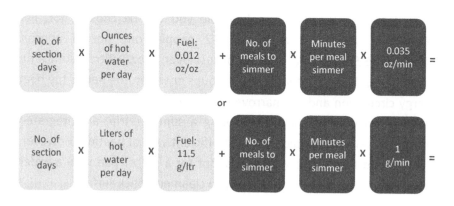

Figure 14 Estimating Fuel Needs

One example for estimating your fuel needs:

Anne is planning 15 days on the JMT with one resupply after 8 days; i.e. her first section is 8 days and her second section is 7 days long. Anne does not like hot drinks and estimates her hot water demand per day to be 27oz/0.8ltr. 5 of her first section meals each have to be simmered for 10min.

Her fuel estimates for section one and two are:

1) 8 x 0.8ltr x 11.5g/ltr + 5 x 10min x 1g/min = 124g
2) 7 x 0.8ltr x 11.5g/ltr + 0 = 64g

So in total, Anne needs approx. 6.6oz/188g of fuel for the entire trip.

In order to keep boiling times and wasted fuel low, always use a lid, start on a small flame and increase as water gets warmer – never turning to full throttle. Furthermore, use a windscreen / heat reflector around your stove and pot to shield against your greatest enemy while cooking.

As a last recommendation, it obviously helps to bring a fire starter – a gas lighter, matches, piezo igniter, or a spark striker. Options that are durable, long-lasting, reliable, and water resistant are preferred.

Pots, Pans, and Utensils

Deciding which kind of pot and/or pan to bring depends on your choice of food and on the amount of people you will be cooking for. For example, if you are cooking for 1-2 people, one pot of approx. 3x6in/7.5x15.5cm with a capacity of just over 32oz/0.9ltr is sufficient. The more liquid the contents are, i.e. soups or water, the better the heat energy circulation and the narrower the pot's base can be. Especially if you plan on only boiling water during a summer trip, an integrated canister system is the quickest, most efficient way of heating. However, if you intend to prepare solid meals, opt for a pot or pan with a wider base. Especially then, choose an easy to clean non-stick surface.

In either case, materials such as aluminum or titanium help save pack weight and always using a lid conserves your fuel. Whether the pot or pan has an integrated (foldable) handle or comes with a multi-use detachable one is secondary. It's also good to see which gear can be stored in the pot while it is stowed away.

While putting together your meals, it helps to think about and set aside the utensils it will take to prepare them. The standard minimum is usually a spoon or spork (spoon and fork in one) and a pocket knife. Particularly convenient when eating directly out of the freeze-dried meal bags or the pot are extra-long plastic spoons. However, if your meals requires stirring or flipping on the stove, make sure your utensil is heat resistant.

Water Treatment

As discussed earlier in the book, it is advised to treat any water in the High Sierra before drinking. There are six options for doing so: micro-filter pumps, micro-filter gravity and squeeze bags, ultra-violet (UV) sterilization pens, chemical tablets or drops, or boiling.

Table 7 shows that choosing a water treatment system is just like any of the other gear choices – a tradeoff. Summarizing some quick points of the table:

- Pump filters are fast and work well even in little, murky water; but they are rather heavy and require some maintenance.
- Gravity filters are fast, very easy to use, and the clean tank can double as a hydration pack; but they are expensive and rather heavy.
- Squeeze filters are fast, light, cheap, and filter large amounts of water per cartridge (longevity of over 10,000 ltr/cartridge); but the pouch can tear or burst small holes if squeezed hard and the squeezing is strenuous.
- UV lights often come as a pen or integrated in a bottle; they are light, rather fast, and treat viruses; but they rely on batteries to work and somewhat clear water to be effective.
- Chemical options are chlorine dioxide, sodium dichloroisocyanurate, and iodine tablets or droplets; they are very light, cheap, and treat viruses; but they are slow, less effective in murky water, and a taste remains with the chemicals. Also: the individual tablet dosage should match your drinking container size: some tablets are for 2 ltr of water and hard to break, in case your container has a different volume; droplets are an alternative.
- Boiling water can only be a back-up option; it is slow, heavy (incl. the fuel needed), and leaves you with boiling water to quench your thirst on a hot afternoon.

	Speed [ltr/min]	Weight [oz.]	Treats Viruses	Longevity [ltr]	Ease of Use	Durability	Cost [$]	Comment
Pump	1.0-1.6	10-15	no	1-2k	easy	fair / long	80-100	Pre-filter sifts large particles, requires maintenance
Gravity	1.4-1.8	8-12	no	1-2k	very easy	long	80-120	Best if hung, incl. storage bags, great for groups
Squeeze	1.5-1.7	2-5	no	>10k	medium	fair	30-50	Hard squeezing led to pouch tears, hand strength needed
UV Light	0.7-1.0	4-6	yes	>10k	easy	fair / long	80-160	Ineffective in murky water, requires batteries / charging
Chemical	0.1-0.25	2-3	yes	80-100	very easy	n/a	10-15 ct/ltr	Ineffective in murky water; virus treatment, but >1h, slight chemical taste
Boiling	0.2	0.4 /ltr	yes	n/a	easy	long	40-50 ct/ltr	Requires fuel and drinking hot water

Table 7 Water Treatment Options

Generally, filters treat protozoa, bacteria, and particulate, and allow instant drinkability. Boiling, UV light, and chemical purifiers, are effective against protozoa, bacteria, and viruses – however, only if the drawn water is almost clear and after a certain treatment time. Along the JMT, viruses are not of concern, so a filter system is sufficient. All options except pumps are of limited applicability in shallow or small amounts of water. However, this too is not a big issue since water is plentiful in the High Sierra and usually very clear.

Water Storage

How to store the treated water for convenient and frequent access is also worth putting some thought into. Two options are most common: bottles and hydration packs.

Practical bottle sizes are 24-48oz; aluminum, stainless steel, and BPA[19]-free plastic are the most used and suitable materials; features like narrow or wide openings, sealing valves, and straws are up to personal preference; insulated bottles are also available – but are heavier and have less capacity; bottles with loops allow attaching the bottle to the backpack with a biner.

Hydration packs are bags made of puncture-resistant, durable material that are placed inside your backpack and connect to you via drinking tube. At the end of the drinking tube a bite-able mouthpiece valve controls the flow of water. The mouthpiece can be clipped onto your backpack strap or lapel for easy access when not in use. Typical sizes of reservoirs are 67-100oz/2-3ltr; wide openings ease filling and cleaning of the packs; hang loops allow hanging of the reservoir inside backpack.

---

[19] Bisphenol A (BPA) is a carbon-based compound used to harden and/or coat plastics. Ongoing studies investigate its harmfulness for adults; internationally, bans on BPA use in newborn products already exist.

Before hiking: if your hydration pack has a plastic taste, mix a few tablespoons of baking soda, 34oz/1ltr warm water, and some clear vinegar and let soak in the reservoir over night; then rinse thoroughly.

 After hiking: clean well and keep reservoir open and as expanded as possible during storage for air circulation, or store the dry pack in the freezer.

Choosing a bottle or hydration pack is a matter of preference. For the first time on the JMT, I used a hydration pack. I ultimately made my decision, because I opted to use trekking poles and wanted a hands-free drinking option. I also thought I would drink more regularly if water access was in tongue's reach, and I asserted good hydration as a basis of endurance. I was very happy with my pack and have since used it on many more hikes. The only downsides are having to remove the reservoir from your backpack for refilling and gauging your consumption. Apart from that, bite valves make frequent drinking very easy and storing the large reservoirs in your backpack gets you far while distributing the weight evenly on shoulders and hips.

This leads to the question of what size your container(s) should be and how much water to carry after each resupply. My non-scientific answer is approx. 67oz/2ltr. If you are very weight conscious, you can go with half, but will need to look at the trail sections ahead of you. Some passes are dry for over 2 hours of sweat-intense up-hill. Furthermore, you will have to unpack your treatment gear more often. You may also want to bring a small (34oz/1ltr) backup pouch to carry extra cooking water for the last stretch while looking for a camp site and/or as an emergency canister.

For completeness sake, do not forget to bring a cup / mug for tea or coffee at camp. I found that a 16oz/450ml plastic mug with a ("sippy") lid works best to keep contents warm and doubles nicely to measure water for food preparation.

e. Medical & Personal Care

For light weight enthusiasts, the following is especially painful. It deals with bringing several items of which you hope never to use them – not once, not for any purpose. Nonetheless, a well-equipped first aid kit is vital in an emergency. Your medical kit should include any personal medications you regularly take, including such that were recommended by your doctor for this specific trip. There are various well equipped pre-packed first-aid kits. Also, hikers have different needs and standards regarding personal care when outdoors. Limit yourself to the minimum you feel comfortable with. Below are some suggestions on what to pack:

First Aid – General

- Self-adhesive band aides
- Tape (sufficient for emergency and blisters)
- Antibacterial wipes / ointment
- Nonstick sterile pads
- Self-adhering elastic bandage wrap
- Scissors or knife
- Pain relieving gels / creams (with Camphor, Menthol, Arnica)
- Anti-inflammatories and/or pain relievers (e.g. ibuprofen)
- Blister treatment (bandages, pads, etc.)
- Survival blanket (silver/insulated)
- Whistle

First Aid – Specific or Optional

- Any personal medication
- Anti-histamines (allergic reactions)
- Tweezers (splinters)
- Safety pins
- Insect-sting relief
- Sun relief (e.g. aloe vera)
- Blood thinner (e.g. aspirin)

Personal Care

- Sunscreen (SPF 30 and up)
- Lip balm (with SPF)
- Tooth brush & paste
- Soap (biodegradable)
- Deodorant
- Insect repellent
- Moisturizer

f. Miscellaneous

The following gear can be just as important as the gear listed earlier, it just does not fit in specific categories.

Miscellaneous Gear	Comment
Camera	SLRs are great but heavy and can be bothersome when travelling in a group; bring at least one extra battery pack; bring more if you plan on taking videos; small padded (e.g. neoprene) cases that attach to your hip belt are a conveniently accessible storage place for your camera
Compass	Good to have; not essential in the summertime as trails are marked and skies usually clear
Fishing Gear	A line and some trout lures are sufficient, but you can also go all out; any fishing requires a California fishing license: www.dfg.ca.gov/licensing/fishing/fishdescrip.html
GPS Watch	GPS watches, as used for running, show you exact distances traveled, speed, pace, elevation, etc. Software allows you to trace your every step back home at the computer and import data into online maps. They are good to have, but not essential for navigating.

Map	Tom Harrison: topographic map printed on 13 waterproof, tear-resistant plastic pages (8.5"x11"), scaled at 1:63,360. The map is durable, small, and sufficient for the trail. Erik the Black: John Muir Trail Pocket Atlas; with topographic maps, data book, elevation profiles, GPS waypoints, campsites, etc.
Map App	Having a printed map is highly advisable, even if you plan on using an app. There are several map apps for Android and iOS; check for recent releases. With your phone's GPS, the app can precisely locate your position on the trail; some give additional information, e.g. elevation profile, etc. Beware of your device's battery life.
Money	Bring some cash for food, stove gas, hitch hiking co-pay, post cards, emergency, etc.
Rope	To hang clothes, replace a strap on backpack, or as shoe lace; not too thick
Shovel	When nature calls; light but sturdy, as ground can be rocky and tough
Solar charger	Solar is a dependable power source on the JMT. A variety of compact photovoltaic panels incl. rechargeable battery and (USB) power port are available. Make sure you have enough power if you are carrying several electronic devices (light, cell phone map app, watch)
Sunglasses	Sporty / tight fit, UV protection, polarized is a plus

Toilet Paper	1 – 1.5 rolls per week; keep a small hand sanitizer in the roll
Towel	Quick drying, synthetic fabric, light weight

Table 8 Miscellaneous Gear

g. Pack & Adjust your Pack

As you pack your backpack, do pay attention to two things: the weight distribution and the internal organization of your gear.

Regarding weight distribution it is important to keep heavy items close to your back and centered both vertically and horizontally (see Figure 15). Moderately heavy items should be placed around the heavy items, light ones along the perimeter of the pack (e.g. placing your sleeping bag in the bottom compartment). The aim is to bring the weight in the backpack as close to the center of your back as possible. This way, the pack's center of gravity is closest to your own, making it less likely for you to lose your balance.

A well-considered internal organization and distribution of gear among the compartments and pockets of your pack can save time and nerves.

 Anything that needs easy and frequent access, such as a map, sunscreen, snacks, or a pocket knife, should be stored in an accessible outside pocket near/on the top.

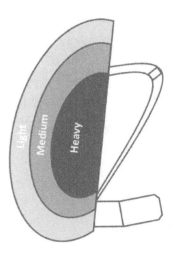

Figure 15 Backpack Weight Distribution

Gear that will only be used once at camp in the evening can be placed inside and below heavy items. Tent poles can also be separated from the tent pack for better storability. Depending on the specific partitioning of your pack, you will see in the first days of hiking, which compartments are best suited for which gear. It helps to then stick to a specific organization.

For easier organization in the main compartment, it is good to use thin plastic bags or (water resistant) compression sacks. They can be individually stuffed and make accessing contents more convenient while providing additional protection against water and dirt. Valuables (phone, keys, money) can be kept in a zip lock bag and buried, as they will hardly be needed. Keep rain gear easily accessible (incl. plastic trash bag, if you do not have a rain cover). Once you have all your items in place and are ready to take off, pull all compression straps. They are usually located on the sides of your pack and at the top. Tightening the compression straps brings the weight closer to your back and inhibits gear from shifting.

Adjusting your pack starts by putting it on correctly. If your pack is heavy, place one foot forward and lift the pack onto your thigh. Then, slip into the shoulder straps and lean forward, pulling the pack onto your back. As you lean forward, position the pack so the hip belt is centered comfortably over your hip bone, then close and tighten the hip belt firmly. As you straighten up, your shoulder straps should be loose and 100% of the pack's weight on your hips. In this starting position the shoulder straps should have a gap of approx. 1in/2cm over your shoulders (however, the anchor points of the shoulder harness will be below your shoulders). If the straps already put pressure on your shoulders in the starting position and your pack has an adjustable suspension, slide the entire shoulder harness up a little and re-secure it. Now, tighten your shoulder straps so they touch your shoulders. Contrary to former backpacks, today's packs are supported primarily by the hip belt with only approx. 10% of the weight being carried by your shoulders. Keep this in mind as you adjust and tighten the straps. Then, pull your load lifters (that extend from the top of your shoulder straps to the top of your pack) so that they form a 45° angle to a horizontal. This brings the pack's center of gravity closer to yours. Now, close your sternum strap and tighten comfortably in front of your chest. This reduces the pack's tendency of pulling your shoulders back. Finally, check your shoulder straps again. The shoulder straps should not be under great tension. Make sure you are merely guiding the weight and keeping it close to your center of gravity rather than carrying it with your shoulders.

7. Personal JMT Experience

In this section, I describe my specific preparation, travel arrangements, gear, and experiences along the trail. It is my trip summary with my good friend Josh, meant to exemplify what worked (for us). It offers only my personal experience and opinion. If you are inexperienced and/or unsure about certain options, I hope this gives you some additional reference points.

a. Plan

First, I researched the JMT and decided which direction to walk it. We chose north-to-south, because a) we trusted the majority and b) we wanted to ascend Mt. Whitney and didn't want to deal with the lottery system when entering from Whitney Portal. I checked for permits at Yosemite online, called-in and faxed the application. I received confirmation of my trail entry date the same day, also via fax. I then made a reservation for a one-way rental car from San Diego to Merced two days before the entry date (Day -1). For Merced, we booked a motel (for Evening -1) near the small airport where both the rental car drop-off and the bus station of the YARTS to Yosemite Valley are located. The YARTS does not need reservation. As we started our trip in busy July and did not get the Happy Isles trail head but the Glacier Point entry, we were faced with the decision of either hiking up a steep incline from the valley floor to Glacier Point or take a bus. We decided to take a bus, worried our packs would be insanely heavy in the beginning. Consequently, I also made the required reservation for the Glacier Point charter bus. We made print outs of all confirmations and marked on a map how to get where and by when. This concluded the long lead items for me, since the idea to our hike came from Josh, i.e. my hiking buddy was fix.

With that out of the way, I had about 4 months leading up to the trip in order to research, buy, and test gear. I'm like a kid in a candy store at a good outdoor shop. I frequently dropped by, tried out products I had researched online, and kept an eye out for deals – both in-store and online. When people at the register started greeting me by name, however, I was starting to wonder if I was going overboard – and I monitored my bank account more diligently.

I had a decent backpack and what I thought was a good sleeping bag, but still needed quite a bit of gear. What I was most unsure about before the trip was what to expect temperature-wise and how to prepare for sleeping arrangements. I couldn't quite believe the numbers from temperature charts, thinking it was impossible it would get that cold in California in the summer. On the other hand, I found it difficult to gauge in online forums, who were the "normal" hikers and who were the "minimalist" ultra-light hikers with a latent death wish. Talk of not needing a tent and sleeping under the stars sounded appealing but also risky. In hindsight, I would consider both Josh's and my approach to be very average / common for the trail and fitting to most people's comfort levels. Here is a list of my gear:

Gear	Comments on my Gear
backpack	75 ltr., rather rugged, i.e. heavy but durable; well-padded and ventilated. I used the sleeping bag compartment for my bear canister – not an ideal weight distribution, but very convenient access. Map was in the top pocket, sunscreen accessible on the side, and the drinking tube clipped to a loop on my right shoulder strap so it was always in reach. Josh had an equally rugged, but poorly ventilated pack. He had never encountered any problems with it, but was sweating more under the California sun and soon faced issues with chaffing along his hips

	and shoulders. Also, his pack had less compartments and pockets, making it more difficult to organize / find what he was looking for.
tent	1-person, 3-season, ultra-light tent with foot print. Packed weight just over 2lb/1kg. I highly recommend using a modern, light 1-person tent over a bivy bag. The extra weight is nothing compared to the additional comfort. Before the trip I was thinking about saving weight and using a tarp if need be. I am very glad I didn't – there might be experienced / passible hikers for whom that is a feasible option, but it definitely wasn't for me. Josh used an older bivy. It weighed about as much as my tent, but since he already had it he thought he'd save the extra $250. Overall, it worked ok. At each campsite he would collect a few rocks and sticks to expand the bivy as far out as possible, allowing more air circulation. This was the biggest issue, as the bivy had a single shell of water-proof, non-breathable material. Josh could not keep his backpack dry under the vestibule like I did, nor could he move around much, let alone change clothes in his bivy.
sleeping bag	ultra-light down bag with a comfort zone of 54°F/12°C. It was far too cold! I would opt for a comfort zone of at least 40°F/4°C.
sleeping pad	ultra-light frame, only padded where body touches ground (head, shoulders, butt, calves, feet) – far too cold and uncomfortable; esp. if you are not a back sleeper, your hip bone will soon hit the ground There are some excellent pads out there; I now have a very comfortable air pad that is 2.5in/6.3cm thick and weighs only 12oz/350g.

stove	simple, 4-arm-foldout, screw onto canister – worked great
fuel	gas cartridge with isobutane mix – easy handling, worked great. The two of us used one 8oz/227g canister per week. We heated water for hot muesli and coffee every morning and had hot water for tea and dehydrated meals every evening. I was, however, very cautious about gas consumption, keeping the flame low, the lid on, and using a wind shield.
lighting device	spark striker – works great and is absolutely reliable, but we also had one back-up lighter
pot	Together, we shared one coated pot with a capacity of approx. 34oz/1ltr. The pot had handles that folded to its sides and a lid. It was cheap and absolutely sufficient.
long spoon / utensils	We both had one plastic spoon that was about 9in/22cm long. It worked great for scraping muesli out of the pre-packed zip-lock bags and eating straight out of the dehydrated instant meal packages. That's all we needed.
bear canister	700cu in. canister. We both used a transparent one with a screw-click lid and bought them when they were on sale. They are not very light, but rather inexpensive, work fine, and double as a seat. They were not bear tested, so I cannot judge the resilience.
water treatment	squeeze filter system. The pros were its good flow rate and light weight. The cons were that the rubber seal between filter and pouch kept getting loose,

	blocking the thread, falling into the pouch, or simply not sealing well. Also, the pouch had several holes at the end, squirting water everywhere and making refills quite time consuming. I would recommend either a light weight pump (can be shared by multiple people) or tablets/droplets. As a back-up, I carried some tablets anyway (weight < 1oz/30g)
hydration pack	70oz/2ltr hydration pack with a non-insulated drinking tube. Along the trail, there is never a reason to carry more than 70oz/2ltr, while carrying less is viable but means more planning, stops, and unpacking a filter - so this size seemed perfect to Josh and me. Thorough rinsing before the trek lessens plastic taste.
extra foldable reservoir	34oz/1ltr. My spare water reservoir / pouch came in handy at camp and should your hydration pack tear. Also convenient for washing up with soap away from the stream/lake. The extra weight is negligible.
mug with lid	16oz/0.5ltr plastic mug with a tight-fitting sippy-cup lid. The mug kept my tea and coffee warm for a long time and had water measurement lines. Great!
pocket knife	Swiss army knife with scissors. A knife is a must. Additionally, the scissors came in very handy when cutting tape / bandages.
first aid kit	I compiled my own first-aid kit with antiseptic, bandages, plenty of tape, blister pads, ibuprofen, and tiger balm. Each evening, I applied tiger balm to my knees and ankles, which sometimes act up. Throughout the trip, I was pain free and the smell was refreshing before going to bed.

silver survival blanket	We each carried one survival blanket that we spread beneath our sleeping pads for extra insulation. With both my sleeping bag and pad being inadequate, I was thankful for any extra warmth. In case of other emergencies or shelter, a survival blanket is versatile and weighs little.
sunscreen	I used one 2oz/60ml tube of SPF 30 per week. I only used sunscreen for my neck and face, occasionally for my arms. Wearing long sleeves, high collars, and other textiles is always favorable over sunscreen. The combination of dust, sweat, and sunscreen gets ever more uncomfortable throughout the day.
soap (biodegradable)	One 1oz/30ml bottle was more than enough for me. Since we only used the pot for boiling water, there was nothing to clean but ourselves and spoons.
camera	Though it was painful hiking in such beautiful scenery without my SLR, I did not bring it. I do not regret my decision, because I know the SLR's extra weight, bulkiness, and fragility would have annoyed me on the trail. Instead, I brought a good point and shoot model, two 32GB SD cards and two extra batteries – all 3 batteries were empty at the end. The batteries did not work in the mornings when it was too cold; keep them in/near your sleeping bag or carry the battery separately in a pant pocket in the morning for quicker warming up. I got a small neoprene case with a belt loop that I attached to my hip belt so it would not slide out. This way, my camera was protected and always in my immediate reach. I highly recommend this.
map or map app	I used the Tom Harrison 13-page topographical maps. The maps are durable and detailed enough to navigate along the trail.

elevation profile	An elevation profile with a vertical mileage chart is very helpful to plan your daily distances. I had gathered different elevation profiles from posts online. None were really great – that's why I made my own for this book. I had set out to hike the JMT in 14 days, which meant approx. 16 miles per day. I roughly marked camping spots every 16 miles along the elevation map and then moved them back or forth a little, depending on the stretches' elevation. This gave us a rough guideline of where we needed to be after each day. In the evenings I would reassess and plan the next day, but overall we stuck to the pre-trail plan rather closely.
money	I hadn't planned on stopping for food or buying anything at the resupply. But after an evening of soaking in the hot springs, we treated ourselves to breakfast at Reds Meadow Resort and got some snacks at the store next door. At the resupply, we did not purchase anything – we had too much gas to begin with and more food than we could carry. After 222miles at Whitney Portal, burgers and a beer were too tempting to resist. Finally, our return to San Diego was free. All in all, about $40 in cash were sufficient for me.
rope	I had brought plenty of rope along that I never used. On the second to last day, my shoe lace did rip, but I was able to re-tie it. 15ft/5m of 3-5mm emergency rope should do.
shovel	We bought and shared a cheap ($3) plastic shovel. It was light, but broke at the end. The shovel could have been ok with more caution while digging, but a sturdy model is definitely a plus. As with everything, it is a question of what you are willing to spend.

sunglasses	My shades were rubberized on the inside and fit fairly tight, making them sit nicely without sliding. Look out for 100% UV protection. Polarized lenses are a plus; mine brilliantly intensify colors.
toilet paper	We each used about one role per week, but each had one role extra. TP is not something you want to have to substitute. Estimating your usage is easy: Next Monday, take a new role of TP, set it aside as yours if you share a bathroom, and check how much is left Sunday evening. Consider if this was an average week and pack accordingly.
towel	I brought a small synthetic, quick drying towel of approx. 15x20in /40x50cm. It is perfectly sufficient for drying off after a swim and is dry the next morning.
solar charger & LED lamp	Instead of a flash light or head lamp, I only brought an LED light with a USB port that connected into my solar charger with battery. The 7 LEDs are very bright but energy efficient. My solar charger with battery, only 3x5in/8x12cm, powered the LEDs for over 4 hours. In the evenings, that was far more than we needed. Only on our last ascent to Mt. Whitney, leaving camp at 4am, I got close to - but never depleted - its full capacity. While Josh had his headlamp strapped on, I put my charger in my top backpack pocket and let the LEDs shine over my shoulder. The lights were attached to a flexible metal "hose" of approx. 6in/15cm so I could twist the light to shine right in front of me.
trekking poles	As stated earlier, I strongly advocate trekking poles. I used extendable telescope poles with one clip and one screw fastener. Make sure to always secure the fasteners tightly. My poles have shock absorbers. To

	me, they are neither big gain nor harm. Well-fitting and moisture-wicking grips are far more important, as are fitting straps and the right length adjustment.
fishing gear	Excited about the possibility of adding fresh fish to our diet of dried goods, I bought a CA fishing license (at a CA fishing store, also possible online at www.dfg.ca.gov/licensing/ols) and brought some fishing gear. Keeping it lightweight, I ditched pole and reel and only packed some line on a spool, flies, and bobbers. We only fished twice and caught one presentable trout. If you are hiking the JMT in 14 days or less, you should have quite a pep in your step to be able to spare time for fishing.

Table 9 Comments on Gear

Besides gear, food and nutrition play a major role. In addition to the suggestions in Chapter 5c *Food*, here are some personal remarks on the food we brought.

Meal	Comments on our Food
Breakfast	We had muesli every morning, each self-packaged in a durable (freezer) zip-lock bag. I bought a variety of oats, grains, granola, nuts, seeds, coconut flakes, and dried fruit and made variations for each day. Each serving consisted of 2 generous cups of pre-mixed muesli, half a cup of powdered milk and two table spoons of protein powder. When hiking, I feel I crave stronger tastes and flavors. Variations of flavor can be achieved with flavored granola (strawberry, blueberry, maple, etc.) and/or instant oatmeal (peach, cinnamon apple, cherry, etc.).

	Personally, I could eat muesli every day for the rest of my life and be happy, but some might like a bit more variation. Nevertheless, especially for hiking, I found that mixing your own muesli lets you combine a variety of great, nutritious ingredients and precisely control your intake.
Lunch	Preparing lunches was the most difficult, I found. We mainly had flat tortillas or pumpernickel either with dried & smoked sausage, fish in a pouch, or peanut butter. I personally got sick of the sausage after day one; while it was nice to have something salty, this was too much for me. Fish pouches were great and I refined them with spices or small sachets of hot sauce. Peanut butter is definitely very nutritious but equally fatty. Though I love a PB&J sandwich, I am not a fan of large quantities and without jelly. All in all, the lunches I planned had too little variety and rarely seemed very appealing. However, I also found that I simply wasn't very hungry in the mid-day sun.
Snacks	We both really enjoyed chocolate protein bars as well as other granola bars in a variety of flavors. Dried apricots, apples, and other fruit are also great, but rather heavy. Almonds and nuts are nutritious and come in different flavors (smoked, etc.) but tend to dry your mouth. We generally didn't snack as much as I had assumed. One snack per day was sufficient, being either one bar or a small hand full of fruits or nuts.
Dinner	Dinners were as simple as they were great. Prior to the trip, I had bought a few dehydrated meals from different brands and tested them on short hikes. They were all edible and one brand was especially delicious to me. There are far more varieties than days on the JMT, so you can have a different entree every

	evening. Preparation is simple: remove the small oxygen absorber, add the specified amount of boiling water (usually 16oz/0.5ltr), close the pouch and wait for approx. 10min. The only downside to me is the price of the pouches at $7-10 each. However, for Josh and me, the taste and convenience after a long day of hiking outweighed the costs. It was worth it, I would highly recommend them.
Condiments	Each morning, we either had a hot coffee or tea. We pre-mixed instant coffee with creamer and sugar – not gourmet, but got you going. Sugar tasted especially delicious on the trail. In the evenings, we had ginger and herbal teas – a great way to warm up. If you are taking self-prepared meals, it would definitely be good to bring some extra spices, olive oil pouches, or other. Our dehydrated meals didn't need seasoning, but hot/sauces added some variety to our lunches.

Table 10 Comments on Food

Figure 16 Organizing Resupply Food and Bear Canister

As you can conclude from my comments, I was very happy with our breakfast, snack, and dinner options, just not with the smoked sausages / lack of variety for lunch. However, quantity-wise, 2.5-3.5oz/70-100g are a good amount of meat or fish. Overall, I can recommend a similar pack list, if you substitute 4 of the sausage portions with jerky, different fish, or vegetarian options.

I sent our resupply package so that it would arrive a good week before our pick-up. We planned one resupply at Muir Trail Ranch, i.e. about half way to Mt. Whitney. Aiming to complete the JMT in 14-16 days, we each started off with 8 days' worth of food, plus a little spare food for emergencies. Additionally, we carried one day of extra food outside of the bear canister that we ate on Day 0 at Yosemite. For resupply, we sent a good 8 days' worth of food, plus goodies such as apples, wine in a carton, coconut water, chocolate, and ready-to-eat tortilla stuffers, and essentials like sunscreen and toilet paper.

We organized our food by trail sections. Figure 16 gives you an idea of how we tried to spread out and sort the four-times 8-day sections worth of food for the two of us. Each horizontal row was one section for one person and consisted of eight "blocks" with breakfast, lunch, snacks, and dinner. Puncturing and letting all air out of our freeze-dried meals, we each just managed to squeeze one sections' worth into our 700 cu. In. bear canisters.

This is exactly what we packed per person per trail section:

Meal	Our Food	Quantity
Breakfast	Muesli-variations	8 freezer zip-lock bags, each with 2 cups of Muesli mix, ½ cup of milk powder and 2 tbl spoons protein
Snacks	Granola, fig, and protein bars	8 bars, mixed
	Nuts & dried fruit	4 cups (½ cup per day) of nuts & dried fruit mix
Lunch	Smoked & dried sausage	6 portions of 3.5oz/100g each
	Salmon & tuna in pouches	2 pouches, 2.5oz/70g and 3oz/85g
	"Carbs"	1 pack of 8 large tortillas 20oz/550g 1 pack of pumpernickel 18oz/500g
Dinner	Dehydrated entrees	8 pouches of 4oz/110g - 6oz/170g each
Extra Food	Sausage & peanut butter	1 portion of sausage 2 packs of 1oz/30g peanut butter

Table 11 Our Food Quantities per Trail Section

b. Go

On the second day before our entry date in Yosemite (Day -1), our adventure began. It was exciting to finally execute on the months of planning. We picked up our rental car (credit card needed at pick-up!) in the morning and drove from San Diego to Merced. At the motel, we took a dip in the pool and walked across the street for one of our last fresh meals. We savored a fresh salad and speculated about what lay ahead. The next morning (Day 0) we drove the short distance to the Merced Airport and returned our rental car. With some time to spare, we weighed our packs at the airport check-in counter: 43lb/20kg without water. Lugging them from the airport to the bus stop (100ft/30m) already seamed so strenuous we briefly forgot why we thought doing this for 222miles was a good idea.

Figure 17 Airport/Rental Car/YARTS Station and Passage to Yosemite Valley

Dead on time the YARTS bus arrived. As this was the route's first stop and there was no one but us, we got front row panorama seats behind the bus' huge windshield. The driver was in a great mood, telling us lots of stories about the area and Yosemite National Park. Much to our amusement, he honked on accident whenever we made a turn – it surprised him each time and never got old to us. With every minute of the 3 hour drive our suspense grew. After a narrow passage in between granite of which we do not know how the bus fit through, Yosemite Valley opened up. Lush meadows lay sun-drenched at the bottom while water cascaded and fell over the steep walls to the sides. At the Yosemite

Village bus stop, we grabbed our packs and walked over to the Yosemite Valley Wilderness Center to pick-up our permits. The rangers went through the "dos and donts" and a few minutes later we were set. We walked over to the backpacker's campground, set up our tent and bivy for the first time, walked to Mirror Lake and Curry Village (info events, stores, and restaurants), had baked beans, and went to sleep.

Figure 18 Yosemite Valley and Backpackers' Campground

Day 1: July 31, 2013 finally arrived! We hopped on the Valley Shuttle to Yosemite Lodge and switched over to the chartered bus. The 1½h drive out of the valley and back up took us to Glacier Point, an awesome overlook of Yosemite Valley and right opposite of Half Dome. There was not a cloud in the sky, but smoke from wildfires near Mammoth covered the scenery in a haze that thickened in the distance. After countless but barely sufficient photos from the look-out spots, and a mental image of the last indoor restroom for a long time, we officially began our journey. Glacier Point is the start of Panorama Trail. With spectacular views, Panorama Trail joins the JMT 3.3mi/5.5km after its Happy Isles Trailhead just before crossing the Merced River at Nevada Fall. Few day hikers pass this point and solitude increases with every mile.

Figure 19 Glacier Point and Nevada Fall

With blue skies and around 90°F/30°C the California sun was challenging our strength from early on and the smoky air wasn't helping. Likewise, it took some time to fine-tune and get used to the weight and gear. Adjusting backpack straps properly and tightening shoes adequately takes some playing around with. Also, my trekking poles felt a little strange at first; timing and placing of feet and pole tips seemed a little uncoordinated. But around the second or third day, the motion became completely natural and the poles felt like a great support.

Day 2 introduced us to the beauty and hardship of the JMT. Headed north, we passed small pines and crumbling rocks on our way to Cathedral Lakes. We were feeling the effects of the heat, smoke, and altitude as we approached the top of Cathedral Pass at 9,700ft/2,900m. But the gradual descent thereafter eased the strain. 5mi/8km past Tuolumne Meadows we camped near Lyell River. Steam was rising from the water, while dear, marmots, chipmunks, and a pheasant awaited nightfall. Dark blue turned black as one star after the other came out until the entire sky was star-studded. Evening 2 was magical. However, as the clear air turned crisper, humidity settled on our tents. With temperatures dropping sub-zero, I lay awake shivering until I finally decided it was time to rise at 6am. As I squirmed out of my sleeping bag, I was stunned to notice it was securely frozen to the side of the tent. The tent itself was covered in small ice crystals, as was the surrounding meadow.

Figure 20 Clear Skies and Frozen Grass at Lyell River

Day 3 gave us a rough start. With Lyell Canyon being rather narrow, we would have waited quite a while for the sun. So at 6:30am we packed our wet stuff and got moving – our only way to warm up. After two hours of walking along the stunningly beautiful river, we spread our tents and sleeping bags on flat slabs of rock and had breakfast. Within 20min, the sun and wind had thoroughly dried our gear and we could continue. It was around 9am; by this time the thought of previously having felt cold already seemed absurd. After a few more miles of flat terrain, the incline of Donahue Pass began. Steps and switchbacks took us from 9,000ft/2,700m to over 11,000ft/3,300m, all in the brutal midday sun. Additionally, smoke from Mammoth stood in the air without a breeze. Getting enough oxygen felt strenuous at times. Nonetheless, traversing the first pass over 11,000ft/3,300m was exhilarating and the view to the surrounding peaks and snow patches was most rewarding.

Figure 21 Drying Gear and Marmot at Donahue Pass

These first days confirmed three important lessons: 1.) do not camp too close to bodies of water; 2.) do not camp in basins; and 3.) try to choose your campgrounds so that you have an incline early in the morning.

Day 4 – falling behind already?! Our campground near Rush Creek was approx. at the 40-mile mark from Yosemite Happy Isles. With a 16-mile-per-day schedule, we had fallen 8 miles behind in only 3 days. We justified the gap with getting adjusted to trail life and some tough conditions caused by the smoke; we were optimistic to make up the time/distance lost. Another approach would have been to alter the mileage, if you thought your initial assumptions on the drawing board did not match the trail's reality, as exit dates are non-binding. At 6am, we began to make up ground. Our morning hike was spectacular. Under the slightest of clouds, we passed a series of crystal-clear lakes that mirrored the surrounding sharp peaks and snow patches. Each of the Thousand Island, Emerald, Ruby, and Garnet lakes was gorgeous and tempting to spend time at. But we pushed on through, non-stop from 10,000ft up and down to 7,500ft. At the northern cut-off, we paralleled the JMT to check out Devil's Postpile – a bizarre formation of octagonal pillars of rock vertically stacked. Then, after a respectable 20-mile-day, we pounded our stakes in the ground and submerged in the hot springs at Reds Meadow campground. Though the temperature was painful at first, the heat quickly relaxed our muscles and deeply calmed all senses. Thoroughly heated to the core, I had my first shiver-free night.

Figure 22 Thousand Island Lake

Day 5 called for luxury. After the amenity of discarding of some waste in the campground trash cans and using a proper bathroom, we had a gourmet breakfast with fresh fruit, French toast, and bacon at Reds Meadow Resort. At the store next door, we sent out postal life signs to our spouses and stocked up on survival blankets to fight the cold. We rejoined the JMT to continue on and regain the 2,500ft we had lost the previous day. While the air was only approx. 60°F/15°C, the sun felt especially merciless among the dusty switchbacks through previously burnt forests. Near a junction, I asked a lady in her mid-50's if she could show us where we were while presenting her my paper map. She replied, "Ya, just hold on a sec", pulled out her smartphone with a JMT app, and showed me our exact location. I felt quite outdated as we continued. The sky had turned dark orange as we arrived at Lake Virginia. We jumped straight into the perfectly clear water, briefly destroying its flawlessly smooth surface. With a small glass of Whiskey, we sat by the shore watching trout jumping, deer cautiously grazing, and butterflies fluttering. As daylight faded, the mirrored images disappeared from the lake's surface while stars drew new ones in the sky.

Figure 23 Late Evening Reflections on Lake Virginia

Day 6 took us over 10,895ft Silver Pass and its beautiful lake with sandy shores all the way down to Mono Creek at 7,870ft. The campground near the Vermilion trailhead was the busiest we stayed at. It is located just beneath the switchbacks leading up to Bear Ridge. We had heard horror stories about how strenuous this section was supposed to be. Nevertheless, as we ascended in the morning of Day 7, we found it quite enjoyable. Most of the path is well shaded in a lush forest and the morning temperatures eased the countless, but steadily inclining zigzags. Around Marie Lake we bumped into a gentle cowboy leading 8 mules. He was carrying gear and food for a group of hikers. After incredibly steep granite switchbacks leading down to Lake Edison, I told him I would freak out if I had to do all this on a horse. He replied he would freak out if he had to carry a backpack and eat dried food for three weeks – his dinner last night was grilled chicken with green beans and a beer. With 35 years of experience going back and forth on the JMT, he reassured us the best was yet to come: "You ain't seen bulls**t!"

Figure 24 Silver Pass and Pack Mules

Day 8 was resupply day. Our morning began in the beautiful pine forests around the picturesque Sallie Keys Lakes. Mice like it here, too. A few of them decided that the cup Josh had left out overnight would be a good place to leave some droppings. Josh had read about the prevalence of the Hantavirus in the area, a virus transmitted mostly by rodent excrement and leading to potentially lethal diseases. After thoroughly disinfecting the cup with boiling water and rubbing alcohol, we made sure never to leave anything outside again and got on our way. After some switchbacks, we took the cut-off to Muir Trail Ranch and crossed San Joaquin River. With some effort, we found the scenic lake and the adjacent hot spring in the middle of the high-grassed Shooting Star Meadow. While the water was rather murky, the temperature was perfect for soaking. All washed up, we headed over to Muir Trail Ranch where our resupply packet was waiting for us. Along with several other hikers, we spread our food on one of the tables and started sorting. On the one hand, we hadn't finished all our food yet, because we had packed one day's worth of extra food. On the other hand, we had sent ourselves too much resupply food. After leaving behind some good food in the cache bins for succeeding hikers and handing out chocolate to everyone around, we continued. We were now approx. at the 107-mile-mark – halfway to Mt. Whitney!

The fact that the resupply worked well was great, but it also meant we upped our pack weight by a about 12lb/5kg from one moment to the next. However, the anticipation of the treats we had just packed propelled us. And the first one didn't survive long: among others, we had sent four fresh apples and we each ate one just after we continued our hike, strongly craving fresh food. Near Goddard Creek junction, we set up camp next to large slabs of west-facing rock. After washing up, we each took out a 500ml carton of red wine from the resupply, lay on the warm rock, and enjoyed cheese pretzel appetizers. As our spirits were lifting, darkness crept in, bats flew from tree to tree, and occasional shooting stars enchanted the evening. We fell asleep outside full and happy.

Figure 25 Hot Spring at Shooting Star Meadow and Resupply

Day 9 – Evolution and Elevation. Our day began with switchbacks leading out of Goddard Canyon. The trail was magnificent, running right along Evolution Creek, which cascaded over rocks, collected in pools, and gently ran on as it sparkled, reflecting the bright morning sun. Evolution Valley opened up to a wide pine forest with grazing deer. Throughout the day's steady incline, the shade from the trees was well appreciated. Switchbacks took us ever higher and along one lake that was more pristine than the next. With each lake and level of elevation, the vegetation and scenery changed. Tall pines were replaced by short ones, then by various shrubberies, until we had reached Wanda Lake at 11,426ft with nothing but a few grasses growing at its edges. After crossing 11,955ft Muir Pass, we had to walk by Lake Helen where all campgrounds were occupied and continue for a daily total of 18mi until we dropped at 7:30pm.

Figure 26 Dear at Evolution Valley

Day 10 lost and regained equal elevation. In the morning, we walked along beautiful rivers and side streams down to Le Conte Canyon. Among lush meadows with deer and babbling brooks, we found the ranger station at Bishop Pass junction. We got some updates from the ranger, especially that fires were no threat to us, and pieces of chocolate chip cookies from his wife. They were heavenly – we couldn't thank her enough. Alongside Palisade Creek, we hiked up the almost white rock of the narrow canyon to the upper Palisade Lake. Here, we invited Keith and Nichole to have dinner with us, the father and daughter we had been bumping into almost daily since we camped next to them on Day 0 in Yosemite. We each prepared our meals and then traded Tequila and fig bars for dessert. Keith told us the story of how he had started to hike the JMT 29 years ago and now returned with his daughter to finish it; a wonderful evening in the company of interesting fellow hikers.

Figure 27 View from Mather Pass

Day 11 was our lunar landing. A steep incline of over 1,000ft/300m took us to Mather Pass and over 12,000ft for the first time. The view up there was spectacular: barren peaks, bright gravel, and scattered rocks as far as the eye could see. Descending into the Upper Basin, we stood-out among the wide fields of unvegetated rocks like men on the moon. By lunch time we had hiked down almost 3,000ft only to climb straight back up again over 12,130ft Pinchot Pass. We shared the peak experience with a group of boy scouts who were somewhat surprised as we took off our shirts and waved our flags in the air - Josh additionally pulling his pants to his ankles. We had done this routine at every peak and pass on the trail, though never in company.

Day 12 – a mini vacation. After a breakfast conversation with Keith and Nichole who had set up their tents close to ours, the JMT took us through two insanely gorgeous canyons. Both Woods Creek and South Baxter Creek were stunning – water cascaded gently over flat rock, bubbled in round pools, and dropped down cliffs to have its spray sparkle in the sun light. We had lunch at Dollar Lake and then only hiked 3 more miles before picking a campsite at Rae Lakes. It was merely 2:30pm; usually we had hiked until at least 6pm. But the setting was too wonderful: steep slopes rose out of the water, surrounding the lakes, while scattered flat patches were sheltered by large boulders and pine trees, making perfect campsites. We enjoyed a short siesta, took a swim, and then emptied Josh's bear canister to use it as a washing machine drum. By now, repacking the food was no longer an issue and by far outweighed the convenience of this method. Sitting on one of the boulders at the lake with just some line and a fly, we were able to land a decent sized trout. We served the fish appetizers along with a small glass of Whiskey while reclining on a warm rock and gazing at the clouds. It was yet another of many perfect moments on this trip.

Figure 28 Rae Lakes

Day 13 we headed on to Mars. Reenergized from our mini vacation, we crossed over 11,978ft Glen Pass as if it was nothing. On the other side, we bumped into a couple from Canada that decided to exit the JMT via Kearsarge Pass and gave us some extra food and gas. With that, we had a fancy warm lunch in Vidette Meadow and continued. By 6pm we were an hour away from 13,180ft Forester Pass and looking for rest. However, the mostly steep and open terrain at around 12,000ft wasn't inviting. So we pushed over the pass and landed on Mars. The outlook was phenomenal. At this late hour, the sun had the peaks glowing bright red. Nothing but red shimmering pebbles, rocks, and boulders lay intimidating in front of us. Accompanied by countless marmots squeaking on their hind legs, we descended for almost an hour until we reached the first patch of trees and level ground for camp. By now all the energy we had recharged the day before was gone and we were cooling off quickly. With little sunlight left, we walked to the nearest creek. Washing up was especially unpleasant in the cold wind. We filtered water for our hydration packs and took some extra water for cooking in our spare pouches. As soon as the food and hot tea were done, I excused myself and sought shelter in my tent. Looking at the map, I realized we had hiked two passes and a total of over 18mi that day. We were now in a position to finish the JMT on the 15th day.

Figure 29 Glen Pass and Mars Landing

Day 14 – recapping the adventure. As I got out of my tent, I was just as cold as when I got in the night before. But the mood quickly brightened as the sun came out over Bighorn Plateau. Scattered, weather-beaten tree stumps with beautiful wavy grain turned into patches of lush pine forests that were periodically interrupted by, again Mars-like, sterile red pebble deserts. Under 11,000ft, vegetation picked up as we hiked along wet meadows. This morning was another good example of how varied and interesting the sceneries along the JMT are. At 3pm we had passed Guitar Lake and pitched our tent next to the lake above it. After relaxing and a quick swim, we lay on a flat rock facing west, overlooking Guitar Lake's shimmering surface. As the sun slowly set in the distance, sending beams of pink and orange our way in between the peaks, we recapped our adventure. Time had both flown by and felt endless. We were thankful everything went so smoothly. With the last drops of Whiskey Josh had been carrying for over 200mi now, we discussed our strategy for Mt. Whitney and got ready for our final ascent.

Figure 30 Wood Grain and Campsite at Guitar Lake

Day 15 – exhilarated on the peak of the Continental US. We got up at 4am, packed our stuff and began climbing. In utter darkness, Josh used his headlamp while I had my LED-solar-charger-combo tucked in my top backpack pocket and shining over my shoulder. After about 1,500 vertical feet from our campsite, we reached the Mt. Whitney cut-off where you could leave your pack and ascend along the ridge. From here the view over Guitar Lake to the mountains around is magnificent - especially as you witness the sun slowly lifting dusk with shades of light blue and violet until it bursts out in blazing orange and red. At 7:35am on August 14th, 2013, we had reached the peak of 14,495ft Mt. Whitney, the highest point in the Continental US. The feeling of joy and accomplishment was second to none. The steady inclines and passes over 12-and-13,000ft in the past days had given us time to acclimatize well, validating the decision of hiking the JMT north-to-south. After absorbing the views and emotions, we signed the register and hit a big red button someone had left beside the book. "That was EASY!", said the talking button before we shut the lid to the register and began our descent from 14,495ft to 8,365ft, non-stop. Though very beautiful, we were only focused on finishing this last steep part accident-free and completing the trail.

Figure 31 Sunrise on the way to and on top of Mt. Whitney

At 3:15pm, we sat in front of a burger and a beer at Whitney Portal, saying cheers. 222mi now lay behind us. Keith and Nichole also arrived, as did Bob, a soft spoken 64-year old who had solely eaten cereal and power bars on the trail, the infamous "Bob-bars". With our first non-dehydrated meal since 10 days in our belly, we got cleaned up, bought a souvenir t-shirt, and took our thumbs to the street. After receiving multiple offers but none going south, we accepted a couple's suggestion to take us down to Lone Pine and try our luck there. After only 15min at the side of the main street Josh called me over, standing next to an enormous luxury RV[20] on a nearby parking lot. I declined his waiving. The sight made all my alarm bells sound and I had flashbacks from bad horror movies. Josh, however, was already taking his shoes off and climbing onboard. Turns out, the driver of the RV, John, used to hitchhike a lot himself and said to his wife Kathy "Wait til you see those guys' faces when we give them a ride in this thing." John was right and our surprise didn't end there. As we sat on the fluffy couch, Kathy handed us a cold beer, fixed a fruit and vegetable platter, and finally a rum and coke. I wasn't sure if this was really happening. Neither was my wife Nadja who drove 3 hours from San Diego to pick us up where John and Kathy dropped us off. Nadja was standing in the parking lot as our huge RV drove up, steps slid out automatically, the door opened, and two bearded versions of ourselves greeted her with big smiles. In the restaurant nearby, we began piecing together the exhilarating impressions from our adventure.

---

[20] RV = recreational vehicle = motor home = large camper van

Appendices

A. Checklists

These checklists are meant to assist you in your preparations. Depending on the month you are hiking and your personal preferences, you can add or remove certain items from the lists. For those who are unsure about what to pack: if you stick to the lists, you will be in good shape.

Clothing [( ) indicates optional items]

	hiking socks (2 pairs)			light rain jacket
	underwear (2)			hat or visor
	shorts			beanie / warm cap
	long pants (hiking or jogging)		( )	long underwear
	long sleeved t-shirt (high zip collar)		( )	gloves
	short sleeved t-shirt			
	fleece jacket or sweater			trail hiking shoes
	warm (!) light jacket		( )	flip-flops

Gear ( ) indicates optional items

	backpack			extra batteries & memory card
	tent/bivy/tarp			photo ID to pick up permit
	sleeping bag			print-outs for all travel arrangement
	sleeping pad			map or map app
	stove			money
	fuel			shovel
	spark striker / lighter			sunglasses
	pot			toilet paper
	long spoon / utensils			towel
	bear canister			head lamp &/ solar lamp
	food			watch (rugged)
	water treatment		( )	rope
	hydration pack or bottles		( )	trekking poles
	mug (with lid)		( )	sleeping gear (ear plugs, inflatable pillow, etc.)
	pocket knife		( )	spare water container (collapsible)
	first aid kit (Chapter 6f)		( )	medication
	silver survival blanket		( )	deodorant
	sunscreen (SPF 30 & up)		( )	insect repellent
	lip balm (with SPF)		( )	moisturizer
	tooth brush and paste		( )	compass
	soap (biodegradable)		( )	fishing gear
	camera		( )	GPS watch
			( )	solar charger

Personal Items (optional)

e.g. a book, notepad, pen, radio, ...	

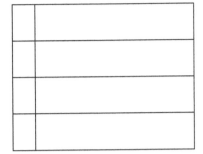

Food List per Day per Person (3 alternatives per meal)

Breakfast
2 slices of bread and peanut butter
2 cups muesli/granola + ½ cup dried milk
freeze dried scrambled eggs

Lunch
canned, dried, smoked meat + crackers
fish in a pouch with 2 slices of bread
dried hummus with 2 tortillas

Snacks
nuts and seeds
dried fruit
protein / granola bars

Dinner
freeze dried instant meal
1½ cups quinoa, dried veggies + broth
2 cups pasta, dried tomatoes + herbs

Other Food Items / Condiments

	sugar			salt / soy sauce
	coffee (and creamer)			spices & herbs; hot sauce; etc.
	tee (no caffeine for evenings)			vitamins
	olive oil			minerals

Resupply

	food (see page 115)	( )	fresh fruit (e.g. apples and oranges)
	sunscreen (2oz/60g /week, min SPF 30)	( )	fresh veggies (e.g. carrots)
	toilet paper (2 rolls)	( )	celebratory meal (in pouch)
	condiments and other food items	( )	celebratory wine (in carton)

If you are sending your resupply with one of the major postal services, you will most probably not be allowed to send fuel. If in doubt, check their respective website.

B. Timeline

This is a summarized overview of the most important things you need to keep in mind as you prepare for your adventure. Please note that this is a generic timeline – depending on which direction you hike the JMT, how many resupplies you plan, etc. your personal timeline will differ. In any case, it helps to start early and be among the first to request a permit 24 weeks in advance to your entry date.

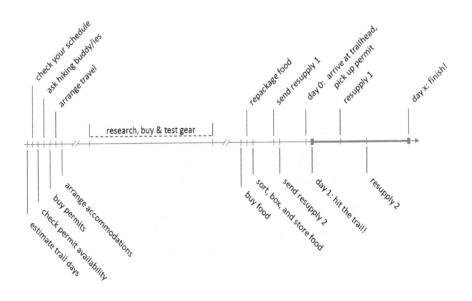

Figure 32 Timeline for Preparation & Hiking

C. Map & Elevation Profiles

As described earlier in the book, there are different ways to navigate along the trail – with (physical) maps, phone map apps, or GPS devices. This section is not meant to substitute any means of navigation on the JMT, but rather give you a first understanding of where the trail will take you. Furthermore, the elevation profiles are provided in such detail that you can refine your general miles-per-day scheme depending on the gain and loss you'll be facing each day. Thereafter, you can conveniently approximate campsites and check how these are located in relation to morning inclines and your resupply spot(s). It helps to have elevation maps along on the trail so you can gauge how far you want to go depending on your condition and what's ahead throughout the day, as well as to plan for the next.

Figure 33 provides an aerial view of the JMT among the Sierra Nevada peaks as well as a compact elevation profile. You can recreate the map and profile by making a pedestrian route from Yosemite Valley Happy Isles to Whitney Portal in Google Maps[21], save it and open the route in Google Earth. You can then adjust view angles and directions and include an elevation profile[22].

All elevation profiles are in feet (vertical) and miles (horizontal). Mileage count starts at Yosemite Valley Happy Isles, includes the loop to summit Mt. Whitney, and ends at Whitney Portal, adding 11mi to the official 211mi of the JMT.

---

[21] When this book was authored, this only worked with the "classic" Google Maps – the "new" one still had some kinks. Furthermore, you will have to drag the route onto the actual JMT at times where the route is calculated differently, also to include summiting Mt. Whitney.
[22] Right-click on the trail route and choose „Show Elevation Profile"

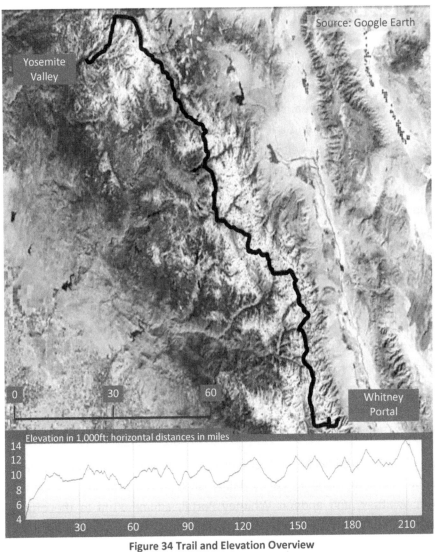

Figure 34 Trail and Elevation Overview

11 Elevation Profiles from Yosemite to Whitney:

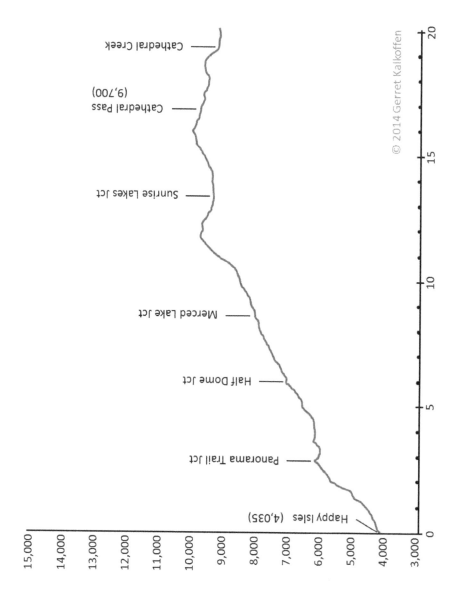

121

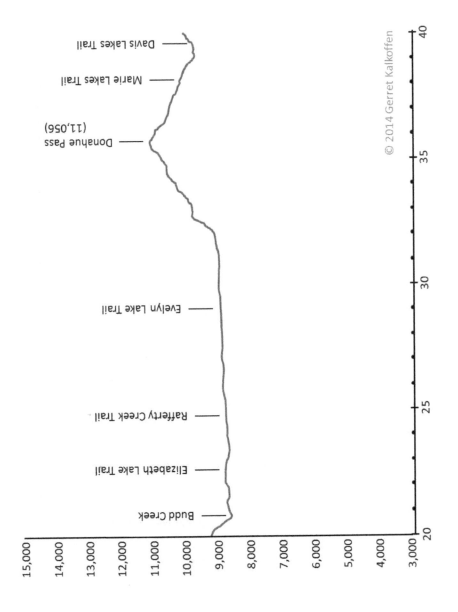

Budd Creek

Elizabeth Lake Trail

Rafferty Creek Trail

Evelyn Lake Trail

Donahue Pass
(11,056)

Marie Lakes Trail

Davis Lakes Trail

15,000
14,000
13,000
12,000
11,000
10,000
9,000
8,000
7,000
6,000
5,000
4,000
3,000

20
25
30
35
40

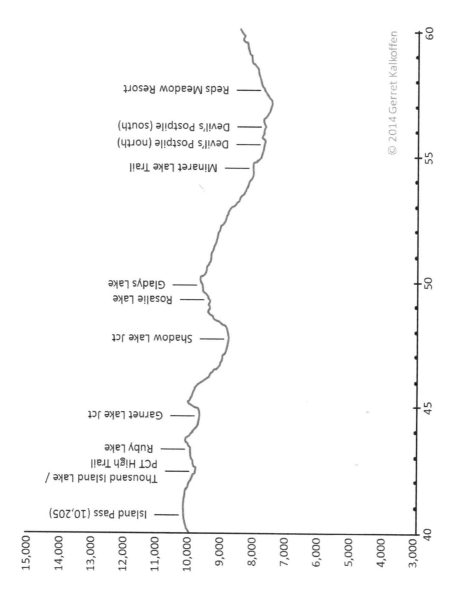

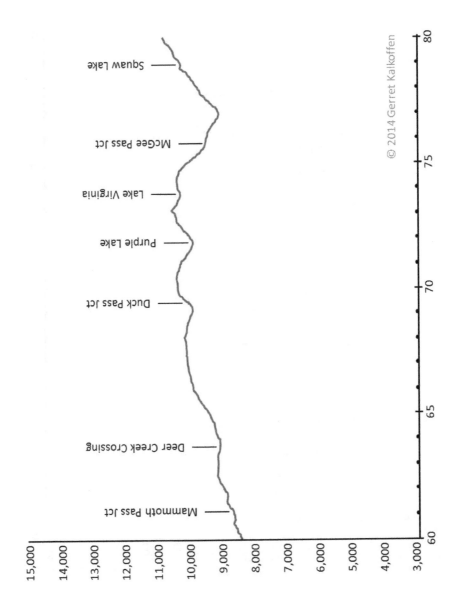

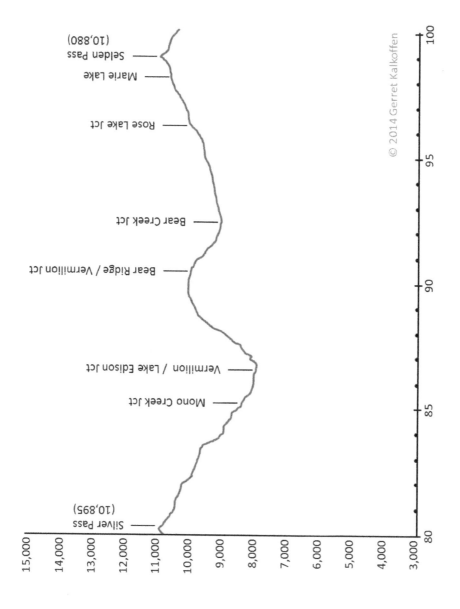

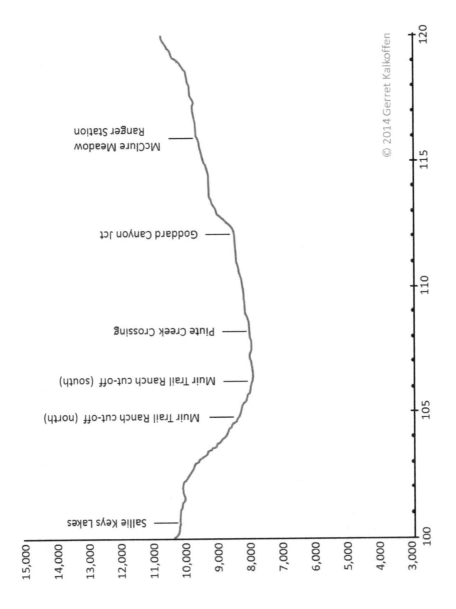

126

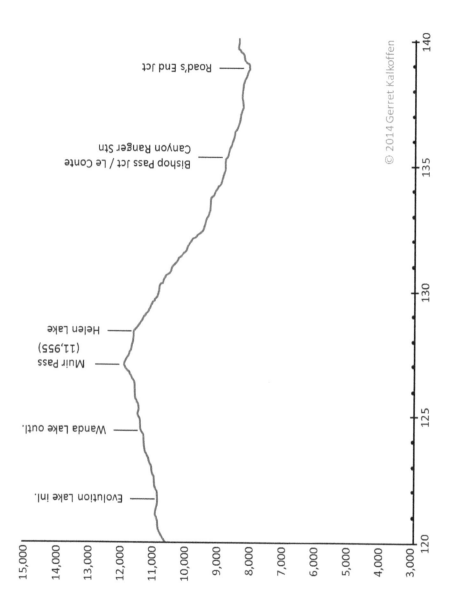

Evolution Lake inl.

Wanda Lake outl.

Muir Pass (11,955)

Helen Lake

Bishop Pass Jct / Le Conte Canyon Ranger Stn

Road's End Jct

15,000
14,000
13,000
12,000
11,000
10,000
9,000
8,000
7,000
6,000
5,000
4,000
3,000

120   125   130   135   140

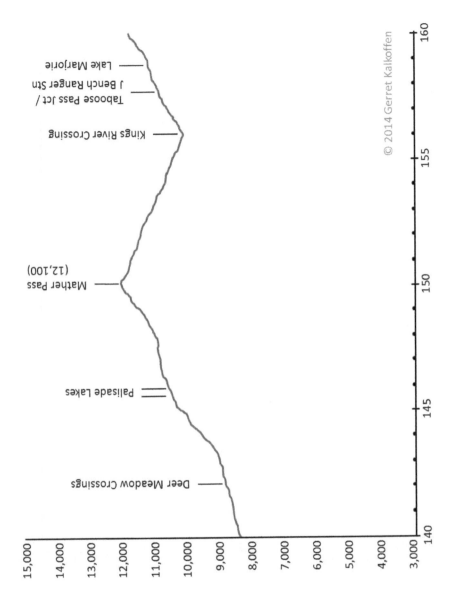

Lake Marjorie
J Bench Ranger Stn
Taboose Pass Jct /

Kings River Crossing

Mather Pass
(12,100)

Palisade Lakes

Deer Meadow Crossings

15,000
14,000
13,000
12,000
11,000
10,000
9,000
8,000
7,000
6,000
5,000
4,000
3,000

140   145   150   155   160

© 2014 Gerret Kalkoffen

128

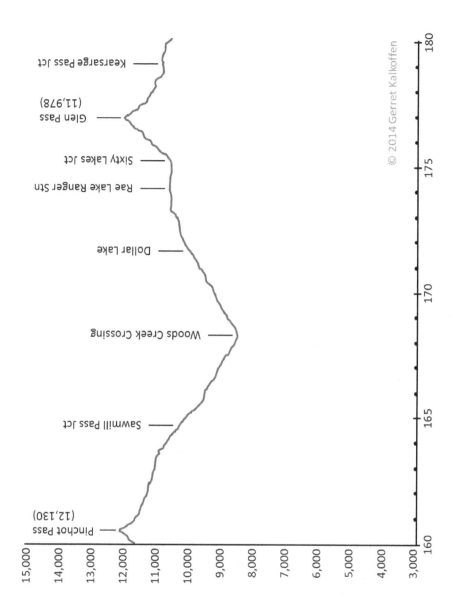

Pinchot Pass (12,130)

Sawmill Pass Jct

Woods Creek Crossing

Dollar Lake

Rae Lake Ranger Stn

Sixty Lakes Jct

Glen Pass (11,978)

Kearsarge Pass Jct

15,000
14,000
13,000
12,000
11,000
10,000
9,000
8,000
7,000
6,000
5,000
4,000
3,000

160   165   170   175   180

© 2014 Gerret Kalkoffen

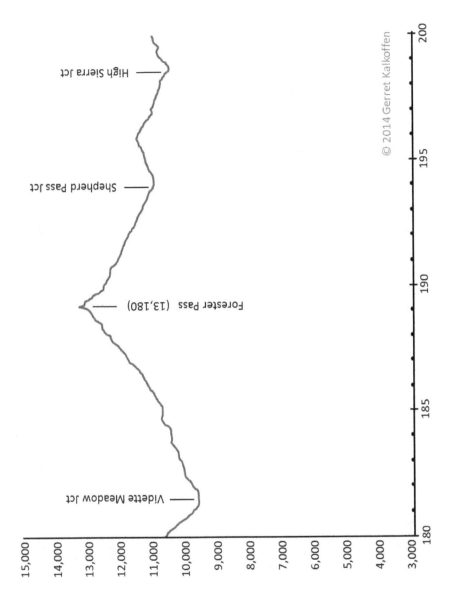

High Sierra Jct

Shepherd Pass Jct

Forester Pass (13,180)

Vidette Meadow Jct

15,000
14,000
13,000
12,000
11,000
10,000
9,000
8,000
7,000
6,000
5,000
4,000
3,000

180   185   190   195   200

© 2014 Gerret Kalkoffen

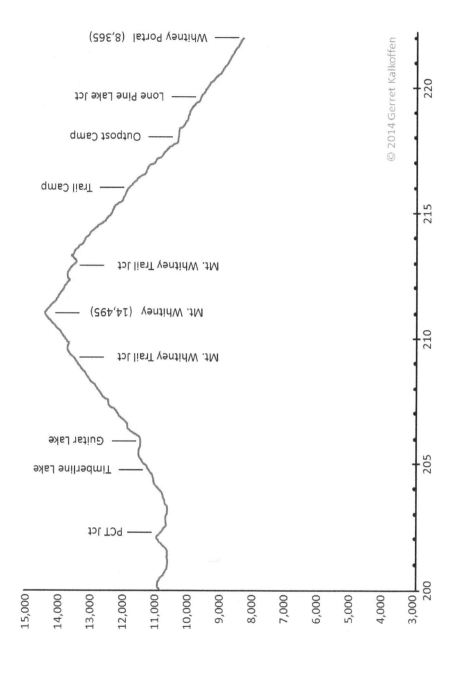

Whitney Portal (8,365)
Lone Pine Lake Jct
Outpost Camp
Trail Camp
Mt. Whitney Trail Jct
Mt. Whitney (14,495)
Mt. Whitney Trail Jct
Guitar Lake
Timberline Lake
PCT Jct

15,000
14,000
13,000
12,000
11,000
10,000
9,000
8,000
7,000
6,000
5,000
4,000
3,000

200
205
210
215
220

© 2014 Gerret Kalkoffen

D. Side Trips

There are infinite lakes and peaks to venture out to. With the scenery changing frequently, you will find a more interesting, beautiful, and surprising landscape each day to soak-up and relish. If your time and planning allow, there are magnificent side trips from the JMT.

Among the most beautiful side trips are:

- **Minaret Lake**
  A beautiful lake beneath the jagged Minaret peaks
  www.goo.gl/waVMDK
- **Bench Lake**
  Peninsula filled clear water near Arrow Peak
  www.goo.gl/yGwrHP
- **Arrow Peak**
  Solitary peak that rises from Kings River to 13,803ft
  www.goo.gl/7K0LjT
- **Sixty Lakes Basin**
  Peaceful set of lakes in pristine surrounding
  www.goo.gl/S3KmUL
- **Mount Solomon**
  Nice peak near Wanda Lake, easy access from JMT
  www.goo.gl/z6VxNM
- **Painted Lady**
  12,126ft Dome of multi-colored bands above Rae Lakes
  www.goo.gl/YYr7dd
- **Split Mountain**
  14,058ft peak; beware of conditions and rock fall
  www.goo.gl/96Am5u
- **Half Dome**
  Yosemite's Icon; steep incline of 400ft along cable route

Any of the adjacent peaks and lakes are included in the JMT permit, with the exception of Half Dome. Due to the crowds in Yosemite Valley, the trek along the cables up to Half Dome's peak requires a separate permit, which is, unfortunately, hard to come by.

For permits visit www.recreation.gov and search "Cables on Half Dome" or call (877)444-6777. There are 225 permits available for each day through a lottery system. Applications start early March and can be made for any day of the season, i.e. when Half Dome cables are up, which is usually mid-May to mid-October. Additionally, there are up to 50 permits per day that are allotted only 2 days prior to entry date based on previous cancelations.

For more information on side trips, check out an extensive collection in:

Secor, R.j., *High Sierra Peaks, Passes, Trails*, The Mountaineers Books, 2009

or visit: seatosummitultralight.blogspot.com/2013/03

Do not worry if you are not planning any side trips. The scenery along the JMT is stunning and the 222mi/360km provide ample opportunity to savor the outlooks from along the trail.

E. Internal References

Marked with [ ] throughout the book; in order of appearance:

Chapter 3a *Permits*

Yosemite Permits
www.nps.gov/yose/planyourvisit/wildpermits.htm
Fax: (209)372-0739
Phone: (209)372-0740
Mail: Wilderness Permits, PO Box 545, Yosemite, CA, 95389

YARTS (Yosemite Area Regional Transportation System)
www.yarts.com

Glacier Point Bus
www.yosemitepark.com/glacier-point-tour
Phone: (209)372-4386

Mt. Whitney Permits
www.fs.usda.gov/main/inyo/passes-permits
www.recreation.gov   (Enter "Mt. Whitney" in Search for Places)
Phone: (760)873-2483 (Permits) and (760)873-2400 (General)
Mail: Inyo National Forest, 351 Pacu Lane, Suite 200, Bishop, CA 93514

Sierra National Forest Permits
www.fs.usda.gov/sierra
www.fs.usda.gov/Internet/FSE_DOCUMENTS/fsbdev7_017679.pdf
Phone: (559)855-5360 (esp. for remaining 40% of permits]

High Sierra Ranger District
www.fs.usda.gov/sierra
Phone: (559)855-5355
Mail: PO Box 559, Prather, CA 93651

Sequoia / Kings Canyon National Park
www.nps.gov/seki/planyourvisit/wilderness_permits.htm

Chapter 3c _Travel Arrangements_

Public Transport

www.bart.gov

www.amtrak.com

www.yarts.com

www.metrolinktrains.com

www.estransit.com/CMS/content/395-routes

Rental Cars

Merced: www.avis.com and www.budget.com

Mammoth: www.hertz.com

Mojave: www.enterprise.com and www.hertz.com

Lancaster: www.avis.com, www.budget.com, www.enterprise.com, and www.hertz.com

Most major rental services are located at the San Francisco and Los Angeles airports, as well as in Fresno and Bakersfield.

Resupply Delivery

Cottonwood Pack Station, Phone: 760-878-2015; Located 25 miles west of Lone Pine near Cottonwood and South Fork Lakes serving the John Muir Wilderness.

Frontier Pack Train, Winter phone: 760-873-7971, Summer phone: 760-648-7701; Located in the June Lake Loop serving the Ansel Adams Wilderness and Yosemite National Park.

Mammoth Lakes Pack Outfit, www.mammothpack.com, Phone: 888-475-8747; Located in the Mammoth Lakes Basin serving the John Muir Wilderness. Spring and Fall horse drives.

McGee Creek Pack Station, www.mcgeecreekpackstation.com, Winter phone: 760-878-2207, Summer phone: 760-935-4324; Located 12 miles south of Mammoth Lakes serving the John Muir Wilderness.

Red's Meadow Pack Train, Phones: 760-934-2345, 800-292-7758; Located near Devil's Postpile National Monument serving John Muir and Ansel Adams Wildernesses.

Rock Creek Pack Station, www.rockcreekpackstation.com, 760-873-8331; Located in the Eastern Sierra Nevada between Mammoth Lakes and Bishop, California.

Pack station info from
www.fs.usda.gov/Internet/FSE_DOCUMENTS/stelprdb5176051.docx

F. Literature & Links

Besthike.com

　　Various considerations, descriptions, and helpful information.

　　www.besthike.com/n-america/sierra-nevada/john-muir-trail-2

Calicokat on blogger.com

　　Great photography of JMT – stunning sunsets and snowy landscapes.

　　www.calicokat-johnmuirtrail2011.blogspot.com

Pacific Crest Trail Association

　　Protects and maintains the PCT, of which the JMT is a part.

　　www.pcta.org

Recreational Equipment, Inc. (REI)

　　Wide-ranging advice and product line.

　　www.rei.com/learn/expert-advice

Sierra Wild

　　Joint website of all agencies that manage wilderness areas along the Sierra Nevada.

　　www.sierrawild.gov

SoCal Hiker

　　Detailed description of sections with lots of pictures and impressions.

　　www.socalhiker.net/itinerary-for-the-john-muir-trail

Wenk, Elizabeth

Detailed trail description with flora, fauna, and geology.

John Muir Trail: The essential guide to hiking America's most famous trail, Wilderness Press, 1978-2014

And of course, visit

Plan & Go: The John Muir Trail

www.planandgohiking.com

for all the herein listed links, as well as more information, pictures, videos, help on calculations, and other posts.

I look forward to and appreciate your feedback!

G. List of Abbreviations

$	US Dollar
°C	Degree Celsius
°F	Degree Fahrenheit
am / pm	Ante Meridiem / Post Meridiem
CA	California
cm	Centimeter
cu.	Cubic
e.g.	"for example"
etc.	"and so forth"
ETD	Estimate of Trail Days
ft	Foot
gal	Gallon
i.e.	"that is"
IGBC	Interagency Grizzly Bear Committee
in.	Inch
inl.	Inlet
Jct.	Junction
JMT	John Muir Trail
k	Thousand (kilo)
kg	Kilogram
km	Kilometer
lb	Pound (imperial)
LED	Light Emitting Diode
ltr	Liter
m	Meter
mi	Mile
min	Minute
Mt.	Mount
MTR	Muir Trail Ranch
outl.	Outlet
PO	Post Office
SIBBG	Sierra Interagency Black Bear Group
St.	Street
Stn	Station

About the Author

Gerret was born 1981 in Hamburg, Germany. Since before he can remember, his father took him along on hikes and sparked his love of the outdoors. Gerret has since enjoyed hiking trips in various parts of the Alps, the Philippines, China, New Zealand, Canada, and the US. With his background in business and engineering, Gerret is always interested in improved gear and technical solutions. Besides the peace he feels when in nature, he enjoys the physical challenge the mountains pose. Currently, Gerret is an overjoyed expectant first-time father and so very proud of his wife Nadja. The soon-to-be three live in San Diego, California.

Special Thanks

I would especially like to thank:

My father, who introduced me to any sport I know how to play, investing much of his valued time. He also infected me with his passion for the mountains that he had developed as a child on various hikes with his father. In his smart but gentle manner, my father continues to be the supreme guidance in my life.

My friend Josh, who had the idea for this trip – just as he did for our first hitch-/ hiking trip in 1999 through southern Germany. Josh never ceases to amaze me with his unorthodox approaches at solving problems. He is equally goofy as well-educated. I am extremely thankful for his friendship.

My wife Nadja, who has always supported my travel and adventure plans, regardless of whether or not she could be a part of them. I admire her strength and intelligence, and am madly in love with her humor and beauty. I could not imagine a better companion with whom to journey through life.

Disclaimer

This book describes physically challenging activities in a remote outdoors environment. There are inherent risks related to hiking, mountain climbing, mountain environment and climate, adapting to altitude, relying on gear, and providing oneself with appropriate nourishment. Discuss with your doctor the implications based on your personal condition.

This book is not a medical guidebook. Information and advice given in this book are intended as reference and explicitly not as a substitute for any professional medical advice, specifically if you are aware of a precondition or issue.

Neither the author nor the publishers take any responsibility for any damage, injury, loss, or inconvenience that could be associated with the use of this book. Your safety and health during preparations and on the trail are your responsibility. This book does not imply that any of the herein featured trails are appropriate for you. Only you can judge what you are capable of.

Information given in this book is correct to the best of the author's knowledge. However, there is no aspiration, guarantee, or claim to the correctness, completeness, and validity of any information given.

Internet addresses, phone numbers, mailing addresses, as well as prices, services, etc. were believed to be accurate at publication but commonly change. Please check for the most recent information. We apologize for the inconvenience.

The author does not have control over the content of herein listed internet links and corresponding websites. The author and the publisher distance themselves from any content and do not take responsibility for any content referred to in this book.

Miles, feet, and pounds are converted and generously rounded into kilometers, meters, and kilograms, vice versa, to avoid unnecessary decimal points where figures are approximated; e.g. 2lb are displayed as 1kg, instead of the accurate 0.907kg.

The mention of companies, organizations, or authorities herein does not imply endorsement by the author or publisher, vice versa.

CPSIA information can be obtained at www.ICGtesting.com
Printed in the USA
LVOW05s1819211014

409813LV00020B/947/P